The GREAT DANBURY STATE FAIR

Andrea Zimmermann

THE
History
PRESS

Published by The History Press
Charleston, SC
www.historypress.net

Song lyrics: Dave King, singer-songwriter, www.davekingmusic.com.

First published 2015

Manufactured in the United States

ISBN 978.1.62619.957.6

Library of Congress Control Number: 2015948738

This book could only be dedicated to one person: my friend and best writing buddy, Mary E. Maki.

YOUR APPROXIMATE LOCATION
IS MARKED IN RED ON THIS MAP.

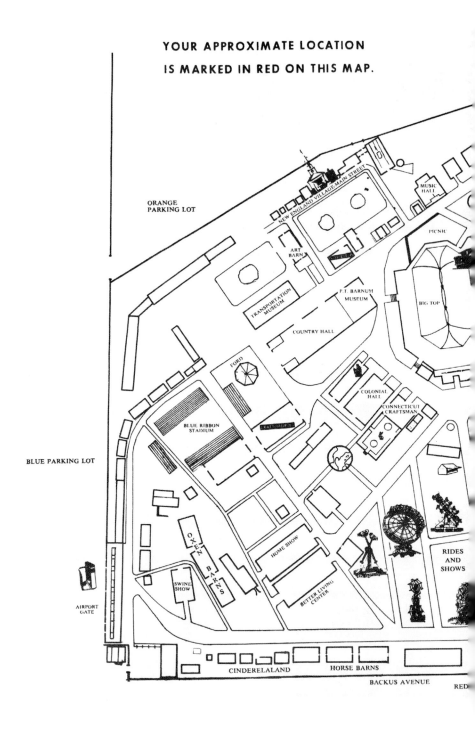

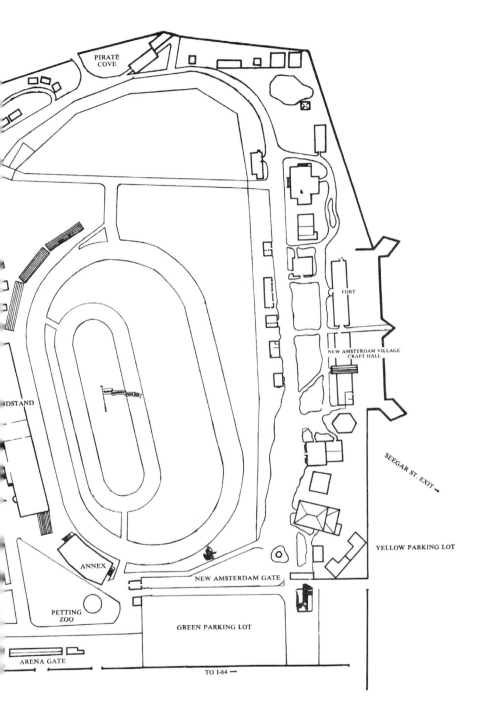

PIRATE
COVE

FORT

NEW AMSTERDAM VILLAGE
CRAFT HALL

DANBURY STATE FAIR

DSTAND

SEEGAR ST. EXIT ➞

YELLOW PARKING LOT

ANNEX

NEW AMSTERDAM GATE

PETTING
ZOO

GREEN PARKING LOT

ARENA GATE

TO I-84 ➞

This map of the Great Danbury State Fair shows the general layout of the fairground around 1980. The racetrack remained in the same location throughout the history of the fair, and during John Leahy's time, the Big Top and the larger attractions he built (New England Village, Goldtown, New Amsterdam Village) never moved.

Contents

CONTENTS

Preface

The history of the Great Danbury State Fair is so long and takes so many unexpected turns that writing about it was like tracking a lightning bug at dusk. One minute, I would think, "Ah, here it is! This is the essence of the fair!" but then the light would blink off, for a decade at the most, and I'd chase the fair through a field thick with fascinating characters and find myself in a different place all together.

It took me quite a while to figure out how to capture this story in my mason jar and make it fun to read.

Another challenge was the factual discrepancies I found in research. For example, newspaper accounts bandied the size of the fairground, citing between 140 and 163 acres. (For my references, I settled on 142, which was the number most often used in later years.) Although these inconsistencies made me a little crazy, I realize I could not have written this book without these primary sources. The newspaper reporters and columnists who wrote during the 112-year period I researched conveyed details that were astounding: the frost-laden weather, the humor of the chicken farmer, the entire pitch of the freak show barker, the names of all the winning breeds of, say, sheep. The language was wonderful and the writing intelligent.

The early historians, often newspapermen, thought to include details on what Danbury looked like at a certain period: "On the oldest streets there are elms which are of more than a century's growth. Nearly all the dwellings are artistic in their design."

PREFACE

Of course all the newspaper clippings, microfilm, fragile monographs, books, theses, photographs, memorabilia and ephemera would be worth little if the librarians, archivists and newspaper publishers didn't bother to preserve, organize and make all of this accessible to researchers like me.

This seems to be the right spot to express my admiration for writers, publishers and keepers of the knowledge.

Also, readers might be tempted to admonish fair management and visitors for enjoying attractions—both animal and human—that, by today's standards, are distasteful. By donning a time traveler's hat, however, they might realize it was all "of an era."

Acknowledgements

I am always surprised at the staggering generosity of individuals, especially those who offer up support throughout my expansive marathon projects, such as the writing of this book.

When I conceived the idea of writing a book about the Great Danbury State Fair, I didn't know the publisher would require examples of high-quality photographs from various decades before it would offer me a contract. I wasn't comfortable putting out a call for photographs without a contract to back up my request, so I contacted some old friends.

R. Scudder Smith, publisher of the weekly *The Newtown Bee* and my former employer, allowed me unlimited access to the negative archives of the newspaper. Curtiss Clark, longtime editor, braved the cobwebs in dark corners of storage to find the earliest Fair Week negatives, set up a light box so I could view them and then squirreled them away for nearly a year while I wrote this book. Newtown town historian Daniel Cruson was another friend who provided images of an earlier era: postcards from the turn of the last century newly acquired by the Newtown Historical Society. The sample images from these two archives gave The History Press the confidence to issue me a contract.

I am grateful to Allen Ramsey, assistant state archivist, Connecticut State Library and Archives; Brigid Guertin, executive director and city historian, Danbury Museum and Historical Society Authority; and archivist and Special Collections librarian Brian Stevens and assistant archivist Jamie Cantoni at Western Connecticut State University for guiding me in my research. I am particularly appreciative of the ongoing assistance of Diane Hassan, research specialist at the Danbury Museum and Historical Society Authority. Diane and I spent many a Monday morning together—me madly rifling through files and photographs and her calmly pulling, copying and scanning material for me, all the while reassuring me I was writing a book people would love to read.

Susan Tomanio, director of the Danbury Senior Center, graciously helped me organize a Danbury Fair Memories Day and recruited people to attend. Catherine Vanaria, photographer and educator, used one of her vacation days to help me at that event. She brought her own equipment and scanned photographs all morning.

I am indebted to Dave King for suggesting and making a brilliant contact for me, as well as Jean Dubail, editor of the *News-Times*, and journalist Robert Miller for offering wonderful ideas and contacts.

Mark Savoia also rates special mention for his tech advice and for giving me a backup drive for my Danbury Fair images. My e-mails to Mark were generally written in a near-panicked state brought on by myriad bizarre happenings I hope never to have revisit me ("Why are my images going completely and permanently 'black' when I open them?"). Mark would always and immediately respond.

One name kept rising to the top when I was testing the waters for people to interview: Millie Godfrey. It was easy to track her down because, at eighty-five, Millie is still very active in the Danbury community, planning reunions for her old neighborhood and for the Southern New York Racing Association, which had its home at the fairground's Racearena. Although Millie didn't know anything about me, she invited me in for tea, spent hours giving me the lowdown on everything fair, lent me her memorabilia, gave me names and phone numbers and helped me avoid a few blunders in writing this book.

C. Irving Jarvis Jr. graciously shared so many stories and details about his father, John Leahy, and the evolution of the fair, all of which helped me create a richer and more intimate portrait.

It is truly the many, many people who so kindly shared their reminiscences about the Danbury Fair that enabled me to write this story. I know how much you loved that fair; I hope this book is a pleasure for you to read.

And many thanks to Bill Brassard Jr., who helped in so many ways—from the final photograph selection to running out to get ink cartridges as my deadline neared. Mostly, however, I appreciate how he has always stood by me.

Introduction

There's a harvest moon over the fairgrounds tonight
The rides are all spinnin' to the children's delight
The midway is crowded with people everywhere
The smell of sausage and peppers is fillin' the air...

So put on your sweater and walkin' shoes
And hurry on over there's no time to lose
I got me two tickets and money to spare
Won't you come down and meet me at Danbury Fair

—Dave King, singer-songwriter
From lyrics to "The Danbury Fair"

For my seventeenth birthday, on Columbus Day, I asked my boyfriend to take me to the Great Danbury State Fair. We both lived in Weston, Connecticut, and although it was just a few towns north, Danbury seemed a world away.

That was 1976. The following fall, I went away to college. The incredible freedom, wonders and friendships that defined that era in my life allowed me to happily tuck away my earlier youth in a scrapbook on the shelf.

I didn't think about the Danbury Fair again until a couple years later when I was commuting on the train to New York for my summer job and read a headline in a cast-off *New York Times*: "Last Fling or Two for the Danbury Fair."

INTRODUCTION

I read every word of that article. Even as a nineteen-year-old who had no interest in history and couldn't leave Connecticut far enough behind, I *knew* something big would be lost if that fair closed.

In the many ensuing years, I developed a love for local history. This interest began when I was a reporter for *The Newtown Bee*, a family-owned weekly newspaper. It was the first time in my life outside my college years that I felt a sense of community—I *belonged* to Newtown, and it belonged to me.

Last year when The History Press approached me to write a book on a different topic, a rather depressing subject, I suggested a book about the Danbury Fair instead. I wanted to spend the year on a fun and happy topic, one for which there was still a plethora of people alive to interview.

Having spent months interviewing, researching and writing, I clearly see what set the Danbury Fair apart from all other fairs: *passion*.

From its inception in 1869, the fair was a private enterprise driven and supported by the sheer force of character and a passion for the event that was unparalleled. While it is true a significant infusion of money buoyed the enterprise after World War II, when it might otherwise have succumbed to debt, the primary reason the fair continued to thrive was the management's creativity, innovation and ability to change just enough with the times.

John Leahy, a man seemingly as large in life as his giant fair figures, was the last of the dynamic managers of the Danbury Fair. After he died, the fair foundered. A very complicated scenario ensued between developers, politicians, the bank and Leahy's estate trustees. But what it boiled down to was there was no one left who had the power, the money and the passion to tell them all, "Go to hell!"

The Danbury Fair was something so ingrained in the culture, something so valued, that churches, schoolkids, merchants and farmers throughout New England spent the entire year anticipating the fall event. It was an experience shared by generations, by neighborhoods, by like-minded people.

Having close ties to Newtown, I recognize why everyone was and is still so passionate about the Great Danbury State Fair. It was a community unto itself. Then it vanished just like the towns that disappear under the waters of a new reservoir.

Rest assured, former fairgoers, the Great Danbury State Fair will always belong to you, and you to it.

ANDREA ZIMMERMANN
Newtown, Connecticut

1

How the Fair Came to Be

Sheep, Hatters and Horse Racing

There are 25 persons in Danbury who will not attend the fair.
They are all in jail, however.
—South Norwalk Journal, *1887*

The history of the Danbury Fair—and all agricultural fairs in America—can be traced back to two Merino sheep smuggled out of Spain in 1809 and displayed by their owner in Pittsfield, Massachusetts. Elkanah Watson tied his sheep to a tree in the center of his town so others could bear witness to the breed's magnificence.

At the time, farmers were too reticent to buy unfamiliar breeds of livestock based on advertising and word of mouth, alone. But seeing was believing. The owner of the two illicit Merinos had expected some interest but was surprised by the crowds that gathered. He realized a larger and more diversified exhibit of livestock would attract even more interest.

"Watson encouraged his neighbors to display their best livestock, to form an association to sponsor an annual exhibit at which livestock was judged and prizes were awarded and at which a distinguished orator spoke on the glory of farming," wrote John Stilgoe in his book *Common Landscape of America: 1580 to 1845*. "Agricultural fairs swept across the northern and northwestern states, educating farm families in agricultural invention and urban delights."

DANBURY: A SWAMPLAND

To best understand the history of the Great Danbury State Fair, one needs to be acquainted with the history of the city and the people who spawned and fostered its fair for 112 years.

In 1684, eight families headed north from Norwalk on an uncharted route to settle a new colony. They chose a location known to the Native Americans as Pahquioque—"swampland." The Puritans settled in the swamp and cultivated the nearby hills. They called their new community Danbury.

Historians believe the hatting industry began prior to 1780, but records before that time were burned when British brigadier general William Tryon and his troops invaded Danbury, a supply base for the Continental army, and set the city ablaze. Existing records show Zadoc Benedict was in business in 1780; he is credited with establishing the first hat factory in the country.

Zadoc had "one kettle, one journeyman, and two apprentices," writes James Montgomery Bailey in his 1890 monograph *Historical Sketch of Danbury and the Danbury Fair.* "His manufacturing capacity was three hats per day. These hats sold from six to ten dollars each."

Danbury outstripped all other towns in the United States in the manufacturing of first fur and then woolen hats. Hatting was Danbury's primary industry for more than a century. In 1801, Danbury exported more than twenty thousand hats.

"In the old days hats were transported to New York by stage coach in leathern sacks containing six to eight dozen," stated the 1935 publication *The Connecticut Tercentenary: The Two Hundred and Fiftieth Anniversary of the Settlement of the Town of Danbury which included the Society of Bethel.* "Ezra Mallory, founder of the Mallory Hat Company, who began the manufacture of hats in a little shop in Great Plain in 1823, used to drive his horse to South Norwalk carrying his hats in a bundle tied to his saddle. There he took a sloop to New York. Sometimes the boat was becalmed and there would be a delay of several days."

The advent of railroads affected the rate of growth in cities; those that were tied in early, such as the city of Norwalk, experience more rapid industrialization than those that weren't, such as Danbury. In 1835, a charter was secured to build a railroad on the Housatonic line from Danbury to Norwalk, but the project was not completed until 1851. In 1882, the New York and New England railroad laid its track through Danbury.

One of the largest and most renowned manufacturers in the United States of fine woolen hats was Rundle and White, whose factories were located on

River Street in Danbury. Owners Samuel H. Rundle and George White also were partners in Ridgewood Farm, a horse stock farm in Danbury; they wanted a place to race their horses. In 1869, they and like-minded business associates, including Benjamin C. Lyons, Joseph M. Ives and Jacob Merritt, purchased property to establish the Gentlemen's Driving (or Pleasure) Park on the west side of the city and built a half-mile track.

The availability of the park grounds and the popularity of horse racing were two critical factors that contributed to the formation and early success of the Danbury Agricultural Society and its independent annual agricultural fair.

Until this time, each county had its agricultural society, and the *county* fair was held in the town that could pay the highest premium. Danbury was host to the county fair many times and as early as 1821.

"Agricultural Fairs are getting to be all the rage," said an 1842 editorial in the *Danbury Times*. "To improve our stock, we must see that which is *better* than our own; to ascertain whether it will be *profitable* for us to raise, or purchase it, we must know its *cost*; to judge of the relative value of different animals, they ought to be seen together; all these are accomplished by attending Agricultural Fairs."

RAILROADS

Railroads had a mixed effect on the region. It was a boon to Danbury's hat manufacturing and all its related industries because of the ease of transporting products to New York and all other areas of the country linked by rail. Conversely, agriculture suffered a debilitating stroke.

"Textile factories began to purchase western wool which in turn destroyed [the] local sheep industry," according to Lynn Winfield Wilson in his *History of Fairfield County*. "Up until 1880 Connecticut, like the rest of New England, produced most of the beef consumed by its people." That ended when the first lot of beef arrived from the West in a refrigerator railcar.

When the Fairfield County Agricultural Society decided to make Norwalk the permanent location for the county fair, Danbury members started to drop out. The general feeling was that Norwalk—and therefore the fair held there—was promoting industry more than agriculture. That didn't sit well with the people of Danbury, whose lives were still primarily agrarian.

The schism deepened until John W. Bacon, president of the Savings Bank of Danbury, spearheaded an effort to establish an independent society in Danbury. He did so with the support of other businessmen—from not only Danbury but also surrounding towns—and the members of the Pleasure Park Association.

This bold move succeeded primarily because the fair was held at a permanent and familiar location and because the racing event dramatically swelled attendance. Horse racing—trotting and pacing—was incredibly popular, as evidenced by the substantial purses and attendance records. The racetrack played a vital role in maintaining the financial health of the Danbury Fair throughout its history and particularly in the very early and late decades.

On August 7, 1869, the Danbury Farmers' and Manufacturers' Society was established; its mission was to promote agriculture, horticulture and the "useful arts." The society would do this by hosting the First Annual Fair and Cattle Show in the fall, after the harvest.

The first Danbury fair was a fifty-fifty partnership between the Danbury Farmers' and Manufacturers' Society and the Pleasure Park Association. With just two months to organize, the society made a public appeal to all residents of Danbury to contribute their best displays "not only of stock and farm products, but also of all articles of useful and ornamental industry."

The first fair ran four days—October 5 through 8, which was Tuesday through Friday. The organizers wanted this inaugural fair to be a big

The racetrack was always an integral part of the Danbury Fair, attracting crowds and revenue. Horses, boats and cars raced here. *Newtown Historical Society.*

splash because its level of success would dictate whether or not there was enough support for the Danbury Fair to be held annually. They were competing not only with the county fair in Norwalk but also local fairs in New Milford and Ridgefield.

To promote the fair, the society offered a staggering $1,500 in awards, or "premiums," the equivalent of $25,500 today. Premiums in 1869 included **farm products** (field crops, grain and grass seeds, vegetables, fruit, floriculture, bread, cake, dairy, honey, preserved fruits and pickles), **domestic manufacture** (men's hats, saddles, two-seat wagons, churns, wringers, sewing machines and "apparatus for drawing water"), **ladies' industrial** (patchwork quilts, hats, tatting, beadwork, shell work, waxwork and leatherwork), **farming utensils** (best two-horse mowing machine, corn planters) and **livestock** (working oxen and steer, blooded stock, fatted cattle, stallions, colts, road/carriage/trotting/farming horses, sheep, poultry and swine). The fair attracted more than 911 entries that year.

The organizers of the fair borrowed a tent from the Barnum & Bailey Circus and staked it on the Pleasure Park site near a rough-board building of twenty-five by forty feet. Here fairgoers found fine art, quilts, flowers, grains and farm produce, including 169 apple "specimens," merchant displays of sewing machines, millinery work, garments, musical instruments, woven curtains, stoves and furniture, as well as a bandstand featuring musicians

Advertising cards were replaced by billboards, newspaper ads and radio spots as a means to publicize the fair. *Millie Godfrey.*

Bartram and Fanton. Displays included cases of the "celebrated" Danbury boots, druggist goods and handwriting specimens.

All exhibitors, except for those with livestock, submitted their entries on the first day of the fair. The following day, farmers exhibited cattle, sheep, swine and poultry and competed in the draught horse and oxen trials, or "pulls." On Thursday and Friday, horses and colts were featured, with the main event—the trial of "Running Horses"—saved for the last day.

Fair management offered an incentive to bolster participation in the horse exhibits and racing events. They provided any horse in Fairfield County a free ride on the Norwalk to Danbury railroad if they were to be exhibited at the fair.

Word spread and crowds arrived in the city of Danbury. Every carriage was pressed into service to transport people from downtown to the fairground.

"All the loads comprised all grades in station and all sorts of nature," reports the *Danbury Times* on October 14, 1869. The "cries of drivers, rolling of vehicles, and trampling of horses was at times bewildering if not deafening."

In 1871, the Danbury Agricultural Society was formed as a joint stock corporation to manage the fair, and all the holdings of the Danbury Farmers' and Manufacturers' Society were folded into this new entity. The company owned just one tent at its inception but steadily increased its equipment, offerings and physical size.

For its entire 112 history, the fair was held at the same location, about a mile and a half from the business center of the city. The society purchased the fairground, which eventually comprised 142 acres.

After its fifth fair, the Danbury Agricultural Society stopped selling shares of stock; it was debt free. Attendance had doubled between 1871, when the corporation was formed, and 1873. In fact, the latter year's tally of 16,510 fairgoers was the first of many years when attendance was more than twice the city's population.

2

The First Seventy-Five Years

A Family Affair, Fires, Pandemic and War

I loved to watch the horse racing and see the crowds of people filling the
fairgrounds. There were two pleasures that my father would never forego: fishing
on the Pootatuck [River] and going to the Danbury Fair.
—Harley Taylor Peck, born in 1885, Newtown Remembered:
Continuing Stories of the 20th Century

B y 1890, Danbury was a bustling metropolis. Its factories produced five
million hats a year. It had two railroad lines to New York City.

"The city is lighted by electric light," noted *Four Cities and Towns of
Connecticut*, a book published that year. "[It] has a long street railway, a first
class fire department, and [an] efficient police force, an elegant city hall, a
flourishing club of business men, a public library and public sewers.

"Danbury is a beautiful city," the description continues. "The streets are
for the most part wide and straight. They are amply shaded. On the oldest
streets there are elms which are of more than a century's growth. Nearly all
the dwelling are artistic in their design, and have well-kept lawns about them."

The fairground, at that time in excess of one hundred acres, was also well
maintained. Buildings included a main structure that was 105 by 90 feet
wide with two wings (one for fine art exhibits and the other for machinery
displays), a five-thousand-seat grandstand, numerous stables, a building for
fair management, three large buildings with wooden walls and tent roofs and
a caretaker's cottage.

Thomas Edison, who operated his own film company at the turn of the
century, sent his best producer, Edwin S. Porter, to film *A Rube Couple at*

The administration building (pictured here) burned during one of the many fires that plagued the Danbury Fair. *Newtown Historical Society.*

a Country Fair on location at the Danbury Fair in 1904. The film captures footage of the grounds, the machinery department, "big pumpkins," a cattle parade and trotting races with female jockeys.

In 1912, with improvements in travel, it took "just" two and a half hours to go from Westport to the fair in Danbury.

Around this time, two Danbury families became closely tied to the fair enterprise. At first glance, they seemed odd bedfellows: the Rundles, who were hatters and bankers, and the Jarvises, whom some still refer to as the Entertainment Kings. But it was a fortuitous pairing that led to the significant development and success of the fair over the course of the next seventy-five years.

Samuel Rundle, one of the founders of the Pleasure Park Association and a hat manufacturer, served as president of the Danbury Agricultural Society from 1892 until his death in 1923. His son George Mortimer Rundle, a successful businessman and the fourth mayor of the city, was associated with fair operations for sixty-five years beginning in 1885. He first served as secretary of the horse department, next as secretary of the society and finally as president until his own death in 1950.

"Mort," as he was known throughout the city, was one of the most prominent men of his generation in Danbury. *The Commemorative Biographical Record of Fairfield County, Connecticut* describes G. Mortimer Rundle as "a man of comprehensive mind and unusual force of character."

George Mortimer Rundle (right) was involved with the Danbury Fair for sixty-five years, succeeding his father as president of the Danbury Agricultural Society, which ran the fair. *Photograph by Baisley. Danbury Museum & Historical Society Authority.*

Rundle had a keen interest in agriculture and managed the fair operations for a quarter of a century. At age ninety, with World War II raging and the fair closed indefinitely by government edict, he found he was the major stockholder of an enterprise sinking into debt.

The other family that played an important role in the development of the fair was the Jarvises. Four generations worked at the fair during the period from 1910 to the close of the fair in 1981. The family ran the Lake Kenosia Amusement Park, a mile from the Danbury fairground, between 1895 and 1926, when everything was lost to fire.

The amusement park began when the Jarvises bought one of the first carousels in Connecticut and set it on Lake Kenosia. When the crowds started to come, the family opened up a hot dog stand. Then they added a roller coaster and brought in a Hudson River steamboat for night rides with music around the lake. The whole family was involved in the venture, which included the lakeside Kenmore Hotel replete with stage.

After each summer season, they shuttered their own park and, the next week, started work at the Danbury Fair.

"My grandfather, father, and uncle all worked there," said C. Irving Jarvis Jr. "They were superintendents at that time—they booked the shows, the rides, the concessionaires. They handed out the permits; they did whatever had to be done. It took about a month to put it together, to make sure everything was rented and to get all the rides and the acts together."

Irv's grandfather William Henry Jarvis worked for thirty seasons with Danbury Agricultural Society vice-president C. Stuart McLean. The two were primarily responsible for renting fairground space. In 1922, William's son and Irv's father, Charles Irving Jarvis Sr., began a lifelong association with the fair as a "stake man" who literally put stakes in the ground to mark the boundaries where concessionaires would set up their tents and booths.

"My dad grew up at Lake Kenosia Amusement Park and started to put together games and things," said Irv. "He ran the little theatre there. They brought acts in from New York, so he had a real background in show business."

Irv's father also invented and operated skill games—such as the popular Chink—at Rockaway Park and Rye Beach. He married and moved back to Connecticut, where he built a home on Lake Kenosia and raised his family. He worked seasonally for the Danbury Agricultural Society until the mid-1940s when he became full time under the new management of John W. Leahy.

Irv Jr. worked at the fair as a youth before pursuing a career in broadcasting. His sister, Evelyn, worked at the fair until it closed.

FIRES AND PANDEMIC

Fire was the fear of every fair manager. And it, along with pandemic and wars, haunted the Danbury Fair throughout its long history.

On the evening of October 20, 1897, a devastating fire swept the fairground and burned down all the main buildings. "By 1:30 this morning," reported the *Danbury News* the next day, "there remained only an acre or two of blazing debris to mark the site of the old familiar landmarks."

The fair was rebuilt using that year's profits and the insurance money.

In July 1916, a lightning strike set a blaze that destroyed the main exhibition building as well as the fair offices. Unable to rebuild these structures by the fall, the fair managers decided to suspend for that year the exhibition of "Ladies Industrial," "Fine Arts" and "Merchant's" displays.

Two years later, a pandemic prevented the fair from opening. Although later newspaper accounts cite this as an outbreak of infantile paralysis (known today as polio), reports of the time relate that it was influenza that closed the Danbury Fair in 1918.

Problems persisted at the fairground. On the last day of the fair in 1922, the wooden grandstand burned to ashes. It was replaced by a steel-and-concrete grandstand that cost the society $100,000.

C. Irving Jarvis Sr. rented the Big Top circle in the winter of 1941 and flooded it to create a skating rink.

"My dad thought it would be fun to have some ice skating there as a little concession," recalled Irv Jr. "They blocked it off and put a couple of stoves in there and rented skates."

Irv's mother, who worked at the fair office during the regular season, sold tickets. One day in January 1941, a stove caught fire, which rapidly spread and destroyed the adjoining administration building.

"My parents were in the office, and luckily they were able to get out the front door because they couldn't get out the side door near the entrance to the skating rink," recalled Irv. "They had to build a new office by fair week, and my dad was in on that; he helped design it."

The Danbury Fair opened its gates that fall, but the cost to rebuild was $35,000 over the insurance payout.

WARS

During World War I, sugar rationing curtailed competitions at the Danbury Fair—and all other fairs—in the classes of preserves and baked goods. In the United States, each person was limited to purchasing only two pounds of sugar per month; the restriction was enacted so we could provide sugar to England, Italy and France.

During World War II, the Danbury Fair closed after the National Defense transportation director Joseph B. Eastman requested that "all state and county fairs, as well as non-essential conventions, meetings and tours be deferred until the war's close," according to the June 19, 1942 issue of the *Danbury News-Times*.

The transportation official cited wear and tear on tires as the reason for closure. "Farmers should not be encouraged to use for nonessential purposes such as these, the tires which are so necessary for their livelihood and so necessary to provide a continuing food supply," he stated in the article. "Nor should they transfer the burden of such travel to public carriers."

G. Mortimer Rundle and vice-president C.S. McLean continued to board horses on the grounds and offered storage space to area businesses that also had to suspend business operations.

"During the war years they stopped selling cars, and the car lots in Danbury put all their new cars in buildings on the fairgrounds," said Irv Jarvis Jr. "My friends and I used to play around in the cars; we'd get in the convertibles. We all had our favorite cars."

With the fair closed, the Danbury Agricultural Society borrowed money to do minimal maintenance on fairground and pay property tax, which was $12,000 a year.

The worrisome thing was no one knew how long the war would continue.

3

John W. Leahy Buys a Fair

He was a stern and intriguing gentleman.
A dapper business man not against change.
—*Charlie Mitchell,* SNYRA: The Life and Times of the
Southern New York Racing Association

John W. Leahy, the son of a bartender, grew up in Danbury and attended the fair every year from the time he was five years old until his death. One of the legends about this enigmatic man is that when he was caught sneaking into the Danbury Fair as a boy, he shouted to his captor, "Some day I'm going to *own* this fair!"

When his father died, John Leahy dropped out of school to help support his mother. He began his work life as a newsboy. Then, as a teen, he joined the machine repair shop of the Mallory Hat factory in Danbury. He soon opened his own centerless grinding machine shop downtown.

In 1917, at the age of twenty-three, he was inspired to open a home fuel oil business after seeing a truck parked on Main Street that advertised the latest technology: home oil burners. This business expanded to include fuel distribution, metered propane gas service, a gasoline station and an appliance showroom.

With only an eighth-grade education John W. Leahy became one of the wealthiest men in the area. He was a tough businessman who rubbed shoulders with movie stars and politicians; he was even invited to the inauguration of J.F. Kennedy. After acquiring controlling interest in the fair, he dreamt of bringing the extravaganza to Broadway as a spectacle that rivaled anything his idol P.T. Barnum could have conceived.

When he was in his forties, John Leahy married Gladys Stetson, a single mother and English teacher at Danbury High School. Gladys played a key role in his fuel business and was treasurer of the Danbury Fair from 1945 until it closed.

"She helped him form, what they called at the time the Jewel Gas Business," recalled Gladys's grandson Jack Stetson in a 2003 oral history interview. "She invented the name 'Jewel Gas' with his initials JWL…Later on we just switched it to Leahy's."

In 1943, a customer who was moving to a retirement home offered John Leahy her single share of Danbury Fair stock as payment for a fuel bill of approximately $250. During this time, the fair wasn't even operating; it closed during the war years, as did all other fairs across the country, to conserve resources.

Leahy accepted the share. He then approached Danbury Agricultural Society president G. Mortimer Rundle, who was then eighty-six, to learn more about who held shares and what needed to be done to bolster the fair to make it a viable operation.

Rundle had more than 50 percent of the shares at that time; all the other shares were held individually by farmers, politicians, hatters and the like. Although shareholders no longer received dividends, they enjoyed the status of being able to share the one remaining benefit—free entrance to the fair. In his oral history, Jack Stetson recalled that all together there were "in the neighborhood of 500 shares."

"Mr. Leahy was interested, and so he was able to buy enough shares from Mr. Rundle to be able to vote himself in as general manager," said Jack Stetson. "He loaned the fair some more of his own money because he couldn't get any more from the banks, and started to do repairs over there…refurbishing the buildings and paving the roads."

Ultimately, John W. Leahy would buy all stock in the fair. In 1946, the first year the fair operated under his management, he formalized his new enterprise as Danbury Fair Inc. He reinvested most of the revenues to expand and maintain as well as bring in new entertainment. His fuel company made him a rich man, and the news accounts portrayed his interest in managing the Danbury Fair as his "hobby."

"He was very, very wealthy," said C. Irving Jarvis Jr. "I don't know if it is true or not, but I heard even the tax people couldn't find out how much money he made because while he was sleeping he was making money with his oil and all of his investments."

Bob Donovan, staff cartoonist for the *Danbury News-Times*, created this clever and concise portrait of John W. Leahy that ran in the paper on December 18, 1956. *Hearst Connecticut Media Group.*

John Leahy owned a good deal of property, said Irv, as well as his own boat in Norwalk, Connecticut, and his own tanks to transport the oil. And when the oil tycoon bought himself a fair, he managed it like any one of his businesses—a very tight ship.

Leahy recognized that Irv Jarvis Sr. would bring continuity as he moved his enterprise from an old to a new era. He also knew—with his wallet wide open—that Irv was a man who could make any vision a reality. And he would do it with great attention to detail, a sense of fun and great flair.

So Leahy hired Jarvis full time as assistant general manager of the newly formed Danbury Fair Inc. and provided him with a permanent office at his White Street fuel building. A few weeks before the fair, Jarvis would move his operation to the fairground, remaining there until the fair closed for the season.

"His office is a veritable beehive of activity," a 1952 *Danbury News-Times* article stated, "where all the concessionaires, pitchmen, barkers and general exhibitors find their way to learn of their locations and to get their credentials."

One of the "giants" of the fair, Farmer John, looks on as John W. Leahy (left) and assistant general manager C. Irving Jarvis prepare for the ninety-fourth Great Danbury State Fair. *From The Newtown Bee.*

During Fair Week, C. Irving Jarvis always wore his iconic "2½ gallon hat" and a red carnation and carried a walking stick. In 1957, the *News-Times* reported that Jarvis had never missed a fair day in his thirty-five years of work. He continued as Leahy's "right hand man" until his death in 1969, the 100th anniversary of what was then known as the Great Danbury State Fair.

During their twenty-three-year partnership, Leahy and Jarvis would build unique theme villages, create museums, develop car racing and water events, engage familiar and jaw-dropping entertainment, build, buy, remodel and advertise. It was thus that they transformed the Danbury Fair into the Great Danbury State Fair, a nationally recognized event.

4

A Modern Fair

John Leahy was a big kid with a big lollipop when it came to the fair.
—*C. Irving Jarvis Jr.*

In anticipation of the war coming to an end, John Leahy began the slow and expensive process of breathing life into the deteriorated fairground. Unable to secure another loan for the fair enterprise, Leahy put up thousands of dollars of his own money to make initial improvements, a trend he continued throughout his lifetime.

"A lot of the buildings were nearly one hundred years old; they were old barns," recalled Jack Stetson in his 2003 oral history. "We had to put new sills and new roofs and new siding. Mount new signs."

Most buildings were painted white and green, a color that persisted for so many decades that people jokingly referred to it as "Fairgrounds Green." Leahy didn't stop at refurbishing the buildings; he also started to improve the grounds and paved roads.

When the fair reopened in 1946, attendance hit an unprecedented 163,500, which was not to be matched until the early 1960s. It seems everyone was ready to have fun.

"You had to be there—it was a feeling of excitement of arriving at the fair and going through the main gate," said Carl Tomanio. "Everybody was in a gala festive mood! One of the greatest things was the *smell* of the fair. With all the food concessions and everything you can think of to eat and drink. The aroma was fantastic."

Set at the foothills of the Berkshire Mountains, the fair had autumn foliage that was only rivaled by the abundant mums John Leahy planted on the fairground. *From* The Newtown Bee.

"We lived on Main Street and during Fair Week it was decorated with flags and bunting," recalled eighty-five-year old Millie Hambidge Godfrey. "People got dressed to the nines to go to the fair, even in the forties. And of course, *everybody* wore a hat. 'Keep your neighbor working; buy a hat'—that was the motto."

Leahy was constantly on the lookout for pieces that would delight people and purchased new figures—sometimes mechanical—directly from manufacturers or ones that had been used for display in the windows of Gimbels and Macy's. Most memorable of the thousands of objects and figures were the thirty-foot giants placed throughout the grounds—Farmer John, Paul Bunyan, Chief Mohawk, the Canadian Woodsman, Uncle Sam and Rip Van Winkle.

"John W. Leahy's *life* was the Danbury Fair," said Millie Godfrey, who knew the general manager well. "He and Irv Jarvis—the Entertainment King—would find things for the fair. If it wasn't nailed down, John W. Leahy brought it home."

Each year, everything was inspected and repairs were made. Even the fiberglass pieces became worn from children climbing on them and exposure to the elements.

"We would have to take everything down once the fair was over and store it all in the barns," said Jack Stetson. "A lot of the stuff was marked for the carpenters and the painters to restore over the winter and get them freshened up for the next year."

By 1964, the paint crew was using 1,600 gallons of paint each year to refresh the buildings and statues. An unidentified magazine clipping stated Leahy maintained the grounds using eighty thousand gallons of water a day.

Over time, John Leahy added many amenities with the fairgoer's comfort in mind—nine hundred benches where people could rest, free parking, free bathrooms (they were coin-operated prior to his management), a picnic grounds with tables and benches, bleachers around the ox pull arena and a paved racetrack so drivers were less likely to crash and fans weren't sprayed with dirt.

Once the entry fee was paid, the rest was pretty easy on a visitor's wallet—free grandstand shows during the week; free music; free parades; and free shows featuring animals, dancers, clowns, the circus, ventriloquists, puppeteers, monkeys, actors, comedians, magicians and other performers.

Throughout the years, newspapers noted the admission for the Danbury Fair was the highest in the region. Ticket prices regularly increased, usually in $0.15 increments: $1.20 in 1948, $1.35 in 1954, $1.50 in 1956 and $2.50 in 1977.

One of the major changes John Leahy made to the Danbury Fair was to add attractions and entertainment for children and families. *From* The Newtown Bee.

C. Irving Jarvis booked additional and more unusual acts. In 1949, Leahy and Jarvis started building theme villages.

"There was no huge change at once. New England Village came out; then the western town came out; Dutch Village came out—that was over a few years," said Irv Jarvis Jr. "There was always something added. My dad would say it was "newer, bigger, and better;" he would say that every year, which was true. But it never really changed drastically from one year to the next."

Leahy was masterful at appealing to changing modern tastes. The *New York Herald Tribune* didn't particularly like the new style of fair Leahy introduced. On September 30, 1946, an article ran in the paper that stated, "Yet, the great New England fair is not the same. Tradition had bowed in many cases to the modern demands for the spectacular and for speed."

In 1951, the *New York World-Telegram* noted one unusual feature that made the Danbury Fair stand out against a landscape of country fairs.

"It is also typical of the great American fair except for one thing;" said the September 10 article. "It is probably the only one in the country that is completely a one-man operation, run without any state subsidy."

The article would have been more accurate to state the Danbury Fair was a one-man and one-*woman* operation. Gladys Leahy, John's wife, was not only treasurer of the fair but also the only other officer of the Danbury Fair Inc.

John Wayne Conner noted in his paper *A Comparison of the 1940 and 1969 Danbury State Fair*: "The famous Danbury Fair has become, perhaps to its own surprise, an institution for the rural education of city people."

Leahy *did* want to attract city dwellers. By the mid-1950s, he was advertising the fair on 180 highway billboards and in sixty newspapers and radio stations, many of which were in New York. Fifteen bus lines also bore Danbury Fair advertising.

The Danbury Fair attracted more people than any agricultural fair in Connecticut and was outpaced by only one in all of New England.

John Leahy built, bought and renovated with families in mind. However, the "Strangest People" shows, Fortune Tellers, Midway gamers and female "Bubbles" acts persisted for many years until Leahy finally banned them from the fair.

Leahy also enhanced the aesthetics of the fair by planting flowers and trees throughout the fairground. The fair, situated at the base of the Berkshire Mountain foothills, got a boost from Mother Nature also.

"The flowers were just absolutely gorgeous—the *mums*," said Millie Godfrey, who first went to the fair around 1936. "You could sit in the

THE GREAT DANBURY STATE FAIR

Even at the turn of the century, thrilling attractions, such as these aerialists, held fairgoers spellbound. *Newtown Historical Society.*

grandstand and see our foliage. Most of the time during Fair Week our colors were good."

More often than not, the weather was perfect for fairgoers. This streak of fair skies during Fair Week was dubbed "Leahy's Luck."

The fair remained a daytime-only event, running from 9:30 a.m. to 7:00 p.m. during Fair Week. John Leahy started to transform the fair into a place for families to enjoy. He created attractions, such as Cinderellaland and a petting zoo, that were geared toward children. Also, he booked more entertainment that would appeal to kids and built theme villages with plenty of room for them to climb and explore.

"I remember the crowds, the smells and all the characters. Paul Bunyan, the gypsies, the shows in the race area, the Big Top. Dutch Village for some reason was always my favorite. The windmill and the little characters with Dutch dresses and little hats, funnel cakes and pomegranates. You almost felt like you were somewhere else," said Jill Austin, who has lived in Danbury all her life.

"It was a magical place," said Judy Menegay Schoonmaker recollecting the fairies and pixies and villages that filled her childhood visits to the fair. "I've never seen anything like it anywhere."

Eunice Laverty, who grew up in Danbury and now owns Bagel Delight in Newtown, said going to the Danbury Fair was the highlight of a six or seventh grader's life.

"The first thing you'd do when you'd go to school in September was figure out who you were going to go with to the fair," she said. "We got the day off and the passes. It was *huge.*"

Elaine Lagarto, a Danbury native, remembered what she wore to the fair as a teen: wool shorts, knee socks and a cardigan sweater over a Peter Pan–collar blouse with an initial pin.

"As a young child, I had a piggy bank where I saved money all year long just for the fair," Elaine said. "It was an annual ritual, just prior to the start of the fair, to open the piggy bank and count the money. My dad usually would then add a little more."

When children grew into teenagers, they gravitated toward the vendors in the Big Top, where they could buy jewelry or leather goods, ride the flying swings, play games of chance, buy beer at the Budweiser tent (eighteen was the legal drinking age then) or just hang out with their friends.

"It was something you always looked forward to every October," said Brenda McKinley, who was attending Danbury High School when the fair closed. "I think that's one of the reasons why I love the fall. Perfect sunny fall days at the fair that would get cooler later. There were times when it rained, but you don't remember that so much."

Leahy was fastidious about how the fairground was maintained and cleaned.

"He put garbage cans every twenty feet because he didn't want the place to be cluttered up," said Irv. "Leahy wanted to have a very clean fair. They'd work all night cleaning it up for the next day and it was the same in the grandstands—after the races and the grandstand shows, before anybody left, the place was spotless."

Leahy created a museum to honor his idol P.T. Barnum as well as one to house something he had a passion for collecting—transportation. C. Irving Jarvis, the assistant general manager, attended to all the details and went with Leahy to scour the region for items to display in the museums.

"They would go around, buying carts and wagons and whatever he could get his hands on," said C. Irving Jarvis Jr. "Leahy was a great collector of early coaches and wagons. He used to put them on all the roofs."

At first blush, the idea of museums at the fairground seems incongruent, but it fits perfectly with Leahy's philosophy of what he wanted the fair to be: agricultural, educational, instructive and entertaining.

"The ag-component, those farmers and what they presented every year—the cattle, bighorns, displays and all the entertainment—was the mainstay of the fair right to the last," said Irv Jarvis Jr. "Leahy was heavy

Many of the attractions at the Danbury Fair were designed to be educational as well as entertaining, including the P.T. Barnum Museum, a tribute to John Leahy's hero. *Photograph by Judy (Menegay) Schoonmaker.*

on education. He never finished school so he had this *thing* about how everybody should stay in school."

Leahy, himself, enjoyed exhibits that were educational more than the acts or entertainment, said Irv. This is evident in the P.T. Barnum Museum, the Transportation Museum and the Sportsmen show, which featured Eskimo families and their dogs or huge tanks of waterfowl. Every year the fair hosted and promoted an exhibit of artwork by Danbury students, as well as an equipment display by Danbury's Henry Abbott Technical School. Right after World War II, Leahy arranged for large exhibits of aircraft as well as equipment from all branches of the military.

John Leahy and C. Irving Jarvis Sr. were sticklers for historical accuracy so they spent a great deal of time creating the three villages: New England, Nieuw Amsterdam (Dutch Village) and Goldtown. Jarvis thoroughly researched each period and geographic location, worked with designers and carpenters to fabricate architecturally accurate buildings and traditional costumes for employees and stocked the shelves of the village stores with representative and authentic wares and treats.

In 1960, John Leahy paid $10,597 in premiums to exhibitors. He partnered with Singer Sewing Machine, the makers of Fleischman's Yeast

Concessions and exhibits at the fair often highlighted the multiculturalism of Danbury. Exhibitors of Ukranian descent created a wedding display featuring traditional costume, food and objects of their heritage. *From* The Newtown Bee.

and other companies to provide special awards, which might have been cash plus a diamond-studded gold ribbon pin, for Best of Show in a class.

Leahy expressed his theatrical flair by appearing in a ringmaster's outfit every day at the fair. Millie Godfrey remembered how she and her husband helped their friend John Leahy get his boots on in the mornings. He polished those boots everyday, she said.

"John was always waving his hanky around," Millie said, laughing. "He was doing something he truly loved and you could see it all over his face."

"He was a showman at heart—no question about it," said Irv Jarvis. "He was tough but when it came to the fair, all of a sudden he became someone a little different. He loved it."

Leahy spent $2,000 for each parade held during Fair Week in the mid-1960s, according to a retrospective article in the October 2, 1981 *News-Times*. He also spent $21,960 to book the Canadian Mounties, whose performance was free on weekdays.

Leahy put most of each season's profits back into the fair and even forewent a salary many years. He was a precise, demanding and unyielding manager. When he bought controlling shares of the fair and ran it as he would his other businesses, his popularity temporarily dropped.

His "no free pass" policy created quite a controversy the first year the fair was open, when veterans were denied their customary free entrance and schoolchildren, too, although it is unclear if cancellation of Danbury Day for students was the school superintendent's idea, Leahy's or something on which they both agreed.

However, as tough as John Leahy was, he readily showed appreciation for good effort and a job well done. He delighted in standing at the gate and handing out the last paychecks of the seasons as the maintenance crew left the grounds. Bending his own policy, he also freely gave out passes to individuals.

"If you did something for him—shoveled the sidewalk at his home on Deer Hill Avenue—he'd hand you a free pass to the fair," said Paul Trudel, a lifelong resident of Danbury. "If he was talking with someone, he'd give them a pass. But I don't think I *ever* heard *anyone* call him 'John.' Only, 'Mr. Leahy.'"

"He was such a great older man," said Leahy's friend Millie Godfrey. "But he must have been a heller when he was younger."

Leahy and Jarvis were always thinking of ways to introduce innovations as well as new ideas to fairgoers and presented these in Machinery Hall and special exhibition areas. The two were like-minded in that they were unafraid of trying something new. More often than not, they were successful. But then there were expensive ideas that fell flat, such as when they dug out the track and converted it to a water speedway.

No matter what happened, John W. Leahy always landed on his feet. He advertised in newspapers and magazines from Chicago to Boston. He expanded the fair to ten days to include a second weekend plus the Columbus Day holiday Monday. By 1954, the New Haven, Hartford and New York railroads ran special trains during Fair Week. This included a daily excursion train direct from Grand Central Terminal to downtown Danbury, where fairgoers would then switch trains and ride two more miles to the fairground.

The fair attracted so many people throughout the region that John Leahy felt justified in adding the word "State" to the official name of the fair in 1954. The Great Danbury State Fair was never a "state" fair in the sense of any other fair that bears the name; it was simply a brilliant marketing strategy to highlight the fair's size, status and widespread appeal.

"Inclusion of the word 'state' in the title—'The Great Danbury State Fair'—was no haphazard decision, made overnight," assistant general manager C. Irving Jarvis explained in a September 19, 1954 *New York Times* article.

The Danbury Airport (top) adjoined the 142-acre fairground property. Visitors who didn't want to drive could fly to the fair or arrive by train. *Photograph by R. Brooks. Danbury Museum & Historical Society Authority.*

Rather, he said, it came about because John Leahy had developed the event to the point that it was recognized as the principal fair in Connecticut by key organizations: the Connecticut Pomological Society, Association of State Fairs, Sheep Breeders Association and Hand Weavers Guild of Connecticut.

Due to the increasing popularity of the Danbury Fair, John Leahy needed to create more parking space. In 1956, Leahy spent $18,000 to reclaim adjacent swampland, creating space to park three thousand additional cars. The fairground could now accommodate sixteen thousand vehicles. This came back to haunt him on those few fair days when rain did fall.

"The fair never closed down because of rain, but it was messy here," recalled Millie Godfrey. "In the fields, the cars would get stuck. Sometimes they had to park the buses on the track because they couldn't get out of the parking lot. That was all swamp over there. In back of the mall, the water still comes over the road."

"There could be eighty thousand people there on a weekend day, a record-breaking day," said Stephen Paproski of Newtown. "I remember my dad and I went one day during the week in the pouring rain and there were three thousand people."

John Leahy had no control over the weather or the incredible traffic jams in the region caused by the thousands of people going to the fair each day during Fair Week.

"Before I-84, the old Danburians didn't like it because all the traffic had to come through downtown to get to the fair," said lifelong resident Paul Trudel. "There were only two ways in—Route 6 and Route 7, and they'd meet. It would be bumper to bumper from that intersection to the fairgrounds from 7:00 a.m. to 7:00 p.m."

Interstate 84, known as the "Yankee Expressway" through Danbury, was built in 1969 at the junction of Routes 6 and 7. The new highway made it easier to reach the fairground. More fairgoers meant more cars or buses, however.

"People parked right in the breakdown lane of the highway," recalled Paul. "They'd just pull over onto the side of I-84 by Exit 3, and they'd park along there. People around Lake Avenue would sell parking in their driveways."

Parents who didn't want to get mixed up in the fair traffic would drop their kids off down the road at the old Marcus Dairy and have them walk to the fair. On the weekends during the last few years of the fair, there could be fifty to eighty thousand people there each day. Locals knew it was best to go during the week.

The fair was a great source of income to locals. Vendors from out of town found room and board in households. Tourists paid to park on private lots near the fairground and purchased gas from local stations. Many people worked directly for the Danbury Fair Inc., and others ran concessions that spanned two generations. John Wayne Conner, who interviewed Leahy for his research paper, related, "According to Mr. John Leahy, the centennial fair was responsible for providing city merchants, suppliers, and tradepeople [sic] with over one million dollars worth of business."

"They used every square foot of that place for attractions," said Kevin Burland, former director/operations manager for WINE AM radio. "I was the morning DJ, and we were in a trailer near the entrance of the fair, doing our regular broadcast from there, promoting community awareness."

Kevin said he would tell listeners what special events and shows were on the schedule and talk about the weekend races, the management and the history of the Danbury Fair.

The fair enterprise became the center of Danbury life for ten glorious days in the fall.

"John Leahy really did enjoy people, as hard as he was. He enjoyed people having fun and enjoying the fair," said Irv Jarvis. "When he would get up at the grandstand during the parade, he'd say, sincerely, 'Thank you all for coming. It's a beautiful day. We hope you have a very, very good day. Come again tomorrow.'"

Gladys and John W. Leahy lived at the fairground throughout the summer. Peter Hurlbut, whose Roxbury family was invited to display its farm produce under the Big Top, remembered John Leahy coming by in the evening while they were setting up during the late 1950s or early 1960s.

"The night before the fair opened, Mr. Leahy used to walk around in his dressing gown and slippers," said Peter. "I remember him coming through and looking at our apple display and all the other displays."

Paul Trudel remembered how fair employees discouraged people from hanging around the gates, trying to get a preview of that year's fair. "Leahy wouldn't want people to see the attractions," he said, "because he wanted them to be thrilled when they went."

"If you wanted to really see the fair, you needed to spend more than one day there," said Carl Tomanio. "It was exciting; it would stay with you all year."

The Danbury Fair always had a large agricultural component, although the focus of it changed from competition to education as farms diminished in the area. *From* The Newtown Bee.

"That's what made the fair such a happy place—everybody enjoyed coming back year after year after year after year," said Irv Jarvis Jr., whose father booked all the concessionaires and entertainers. "The same people would come and join the fair whether they were selling popcorn or had an act; they would always come back to the fair. And they'd come back before the fair ended and say, 'I'd like to do it again next year.'"

"People couldn't wait to get to Danbury; it was like going on vacation," he said. "'Hey, we're going to run a concession again over at Danbury Fair. I'm going to bring my apples over there, I'm going to bring the cow over…'"

5

The Three Villages

New England, Goldtown and New Amsterdam

They would get off the buses from New York and put their order in to make sure they didn't run out…They couldn't make pies fast enough.
—*C. Irving Jarvis Jr.*

The most significant change to the fairground John Leahy made was to add three expansive, historically accurate and lively "villages" that visitors were invited to explore—New England Village, Goldtown Western Village and New/Nieuw Amsterdam, or "Dutch," Village.

The theme areas were built about five years apart, often using the talents of resident carpenters and artists to make buildings, gardens and figures. Unlike static displays of the time, Leahy enlivened his villages with musicians, food, dancing and actors who regularly "robbed the bank" or moseyed into town with the prospecting tools hanging on his donkey.

The settings were so fabulous, a rumor later spread that perhaps Walt Disney had come to the Danbury Fair and been inspired to create his own magical theme parks.

NEW ENGLAND VILLAGE

The first theme town, New England Village, started to take shape in 1949 when John Leahy bought an advertising display at Grand Central Terminal. The display was a grand replica of an idealized Main Street in New England.

After John Leahy bought Main Street New England, an advertising display set up in Grand Central Terminal, he expanded the storefronts to be real buildings and set them along a pond. *Photograph by Judy (Menegay) Schoonmaker.*

The row of shallow wooden buildings that formed the street was a way for the New Haven Railroad to encourage travel to Connecticut for pleasure.

After the promotion, Leahy purchased and enhanced the structures and created true buildings behind the façades. He then fashioned a bucolic colonial setting to go with it. New England Village was the only one of the three to have its central construct conceived by someone unrelated to the fair.

The buildings that composed the Main Street included a church where services were held each day of the fair, a wool-spinning center, a theater, a mineral museum, a drugstore and a country store.

"Everything was open; there was no price to get in," Brenda McKinley said. "You could really spend all day exploring. We didn't go on rides much, we were saving our money to buy candy!"

Brenda enjoyed visiting the one-room schoolhouse with its little desks and slates. Although none of the villages at the fair had docents, there were sometimes figures dressed according to the theme.

Two barns were built, and visitors found chickens and other live animals residing here. Being a smart businessman, Leahy partnered with Borden Company to feature its famous bovine, Elsie the Cow.

THE GREAT DANBURY STATE FAIR

Above: The Barnyard and the paddleboat ride around the pond and islands attracted the young, and the plethora of park benches attracted the weary. *Photograph by Judy (Menegay) Schoonmaker.*

Left: Demonstrations of handicrafts such as tatting, portraiture, glass blowing, blacksmithing and spinning were among the many sights visitors could enjoy at the fair. *From* The Newtown Bee.

The backdrop to New England Village was the fall foliage of the hills of Danbury. This scene was reflected in a large pond excavated in front of Main Street. The shore was lined with benches that provided a respite for fairgoers; John Leahy felt it was important to offer a quieter and beautiful setting in which to relax for a moment. In 1957, he purchased a paddlewheel boat and Captain Nick Fornoro offered fairgoers rides around the pond and two little islands therein.

Inside each of the buildings, visitors would find something to delight them. All manner of things were offered for sale at the Country Store, most of which even a youth could afford.

"You could buy candy by the pound—the root beer sticks, licorice," said Brenda McKinley, who grew up in Danbury. "So we'd always fill up little bags of candy that we'd be munching on all day."

Art and domestic work were displayed and judged in a barn in New England Village. Those who ventured into the Spinning Center could see Angora spun into yarn. They could then buy articles woven or knitted from this yarn.

GOLDTOWN WESTERN VILLAGE

In 1955, C. Irving Jarvis considered what to do with the area known as Church Row, a set of permanent buildings local churches rented to sell their specialty foods. Times had changed, and the churches no longer found it viable to have food concessions at the fair.

"My dad said, 'Let's make a western town because we don't have anything like that," recalled Irv Jr. "They actually made a theme park before theme parks."

The Entertainment King took his cue from western radio shows and the new television show *Gunsmoke*. So he set about creating a Wild West town set in the era of the gold rush.

The town was full of music, bandits and miners with mules. A blacksmith plied his trade, the general store sold goods and the stagecoach opened its door to all who had spare change to pay for a ride. Fairgoers could visit the dentist; the sheriff's office and jail, where famous criminals were often incarcerated; or stop by the local saloon to hear the piano player.

"In the saloon they'd have people sitting at the bar drinking. Everything was animated," said lifelong Danbury resident Paul Trudel. "People

The year after Goldtown opened, John Leahy added a sluiceway so the adventurous could pan for pyrite "gold." *Danbury Museum and Historical Society Authority.*

looked like cowboys from the day, and they had six-shooter guns on, and there was a guy sitting in the chair outside."

"Once in a while you hear a shot and somebody comes rolling out onto the road," said Millie Godfrey. "And they've had a holdup!"

Paul recalled at high noon there was always a gunfight at the OK Corral. Two gunfighters would walk down the street toward each other, and only one would be left standing. He also remembered bank robberies.

"And a train robbery. You could go on the train," he said. "You'd be sitting in the seats, and all of a sudden, they'd come with the guns, and the bandanas over their faces. It was a real show!"

The second year, a sluiceway was added to Goldtown. Leahy hired "old-timers" to show visitors how to use the sixteen-inch sieves/pans and try their luck as miners. The reward, however, was not real gold; it was pyrite—"fool's gold."

"They'd give you a little packet, and you could put your gold nuggets in it and keep it," recalled Paul Trudel.

Another addition that year was the Goldtown Music Hall with two hundred seats and continual music. In later years, musicians performed in a train car with its sliding side doors opened.

"Pepsi sponsored it, so it was called Pepsi Goldtown the first year," recalled Marlene Patren, who, as sixth grader, performed on stage that year. "They had the Goldtown Dancers. [I] and five or six high school girls danced—the high school girls did sort of a cancan, and then I did a solo."

Marlene and the other girls, who attended the Ona-May School of Dance in Danbury, were paid for their performances. They wore what Marlene calls "old-time saloon costumes": big hats with feathers that tied around their chins, bustier outfits and fishnet stockings. They performed twice a day and were in the daily parade. Marlene, who a few years later was Queen of the Danbury Fair, danced and sang a solo, "I'm Only a Bird in a Gilded Cage."

The Music Hall in Goldtown Western Village opened in 1956 and was sponsored by Pepsi-Cola that first year. *Millie Godfrey.*

"You felt special. You know, twelve years old and you're in the parade and you're dancing in Goldtown," she said. "The fair was a *big* deal for Danbury."

NIEUW/NEW AMSTERDAM VILLAGE

In a move to attract more New Yorkers, especially those from the city, John Leahy and C. Irving Jarvis created a village that portrayed the Dutch settlement of lower Manhattan during the period 1626–64. They hired designer Mark Isselee to build thirty-five permanent buildings—authentic Dutch architecture— on five acres where the horse barns had been. After landscaping and filling it with all sorts of unexpected delights, they opened Nieuw Amsterdam in 1960, the year New York City commemorated its tercentennial.

New Amsterdam Dutch Village was the last historical town John Leahy and C. Irving Jarvis built. It boasted thirty-five buildings, a bowling green and a windmill on five acres. *Millie Godfrey.*

"They put up a windmill and had everybody in costumes in Dutch Village," said C. Irving Jarvis Jr. "That was a very popular area."

The idea was to show how the Dutch culture influenced our country; it introduced the first lawyer, minister and schoolteacher and also built the first schoolhouse and fire department. True to John Leahy's goals for all of his villages, Nieuw Amsterdam was to be educational and historical but entertaining as well.

After spending a few years researching the history of the Dutch settlement in preparation of building the village on the fairground, C. Irving Jarvis Sr. was lauded as one of the country's leading authorities on the subject.

Jarvis and Leahy really outdid themselves.

The litany of buildings is testament to the scope of this effort: a city hall, an authentic Dutch home, a mock windmill, a bowling green, a blacksmith, glass-blowers, candy makers, a display of Dutch art, a Dutch restaurant, a general store stocked with wooden shoes and other native goods, a Dutch bakery, a sheep barn, a Dutch Reform Church and Fort New Amsterdam replete with barracks, parapet and dungeon.

No one connected with the fair would comment on the cost of creating Nieuw Amsterdam, but the *New-Times* estimated it was "in the six-figure

Fort New Amsterdam, Dutch apple pies and funnel cakes, native folk singers and swinging bells were some of the memorable highlights of Dutch Village. *From* The Newtown Bee.

Figures made from fiberglass or celastic (a German product similar to papier mâché) populated all three villages. Some were realistic, like the boy with his finger in the dike, and others whimsical. *From* The Newtown Bee.

bracket." If the cost were, say, $100,000 in 1960, that value would be $800,000 in today's dollars.

For sixteen fair seasons, Mieka Michaels, who is of Dutch descent and speaks the language fluently, performed in New Amsterdam Village singing Dutch folksongs with the band. In the oral history *Redding Remembered*, she recalled how she would dress in a traditional costume and wear her hair in braids. Mieka also worked a booth at the fair for the Netherlands Tourist Office and was a representative of Monitor Records who produced her album *Greetings from Holland*.

Dutch Village was filled with whimsical and legendary figures that would become iconic of John Leahy's fair. Dutch figures greeted visitors in traditional garb, little faeries and elves landed on roofs, Ichabod Crane and the Headless Horseman raced through the woods there; a giant Rip Van Winkle snoozed serenely.

Twenty-seven working Dutch fireplaces warmed the village, as did the "Dutch" apple pie that came out of the beehive oven.

"Dutch Village had the best Dutch apple pie," recalled Paul Trudel. "You got a big warm piece and a scoop of ice cream on top for a quarter."

Paul wasn't the only one who loved that pie. The first few years that pies were offered in Nieuw Amsterdam Village, they ran out; one year, they sold a record fifty thousand.

"They would go to the supermarkets to buy Table Talk pies," said Irv Jarvis. "They had cartons and cartons. They had cartons higher than the building when they piled them up; and they used them all. They ran out of pies almost in all of Connecticut—they couldn't find enough pies the first few years."

Irv's sister, Evelyn Hutwohl; her husband, Kenneth; and their daughter Christine were the ones in charge of this concession.

"They would put the pies in the 'Dutch' oven—I don't know if it really was, or not—warm them up, put ice cream on it and sell it. People would even buy it without it being warm," said Irv. "That was a goldmine."

6

Food, Glorious Fair Food!

My nephew was working at the Sugar Daddy stand and, when they would run out…people would shake the stand until they brought more. It was a little round yellow building right outside the Big Top.
—JoAnn Schofield, Danbury native

The topic of food *always* comes to mind when people reminisce about the Great Danbury State Fair. Often, it's the first thing people mention.

That is testament to the lasting power of the fair's tasty and unusual offerings served up in fairy-tale proportions.

"Whenever I smell sausage and peppers, I think of the fair," said Eunice Laverty, who attended Catholic school in Danbury. Danbury Day was always on a Friday, and the lure of sausage and peppers was so well known to the church fathers that special dispensation was granted for eating meat on Friday.

"But just for that day, and only at the fair," recalls David Coehlo, who also was raised Catholic in Danbury.

Now this dietary practice is more lenient and exercised mostly during Lent. But at the time, said Eunice, without that special dispensation you would *never* eat meat on Friday. "NOT [even] if anybody FORCED IT DOWN YOU! NO!" she said. "None of my friends would have. And we were pretty cool; we weren't dorky or anything. We would NEVER have eaten meat on Friday."

"A lot of Danbury people would take their vacation and work at the fair," said Paul Trudel, a Danbury native. "Some of them would make twice as

No Danbury Fair experience was complete without a Bob Maxwell's Walk Away Sundae, not even if you had a button made with your name on it. *Danbury Museum and Historical Society Authority.*

much a week working at the fair as they did in their weekly pay [because] the stands were so busy. You'd need three or four or five people there—like the sausage and pepper stand."

"Zarcone's was always around the back side of the Big Top," recalled Judy Menegay Schoonmaker. It was her favorite food and you could smell it as soon as you crossed through the main entrance into the fairground.

Brenda McKinley remembers the list of fair "must eats" that she and her teenage friends had, including the famous Bob Maxwell's Walk Away Sundaes.

THE GREAT DANBURY STATE FAIR

If you weren't lucky enough to have had a Walk Away Sundae during Fair Week, this is what you missed: a hand-cut rectangle of ice cream on a cone with its top dipped in chocolate and then rolled in nuts and finished with a cherry. You didn't need a spoon, and you didn't need to sit down to eat it. You just walked—or ran—away with it and didn't share.

Also on Brenda's list was "fresh apple cider—there was a press right there, doughnuts and ridiculously giant candies, like Charleston Chews and Sugar Daddy's on a stick so big kids could hardly get an end into their mouth to bite with their arm stretched out!"

Fried food was also a big hit—the funnel cakes, the fried dough, the amazing and irresistible homemade French fries.

"There was a lot of food at the fair that I had never tasted before, such as [a] calzone," said Geno Piacentini.

"John Leahy went down to the 1964 World's Fair and talked to the guy at the French Fried Ice Cream stand; he sold French fries with ice cream on top," recalls Carl J. Tomanio. "He brought the guy and his stand up to the Danbury Fair for 1964 and 1965."

For months prior to the fair, Elaine Legarto could smell the aroma of peppers, onions, sausage and meatballs filling her sister's home. Her sister and her sister's husband helped operate the fair concession Novella's Diner.

"I was privy to all the hard work it took to run such a concession stand," she said.

During her high school and college years, Judy Schoonmaker worked at both the apple pie and the turkey booths, two affiliated concessions that had been at the fair as long as she could remember. She would chop things up in the turkey concession before heading over to work the apple pie stand.

"Turkey and rice soup was their big thing, but they also had turkey legs and turkey sandwiches," she said. "The turkey place had ovens and big stoves to heat the soup up. It was good food. I was glad I was affiliated with both of them because we got free lunches!"

The hot apple pie concession where Judy worked was right in front of the Big Top; the turkey booth was around the corner. She spent all day slicing and serving pies à la mode, until they ran out, which they often did on weekends.

"It was busy!" Judy said. "They had premade six-inch pies they'd cook right there so you would smell that hot apple pie. You'd get a quarter of a pie with a scoop of ice cream on top of it. It was great!"

The chef takes a break at one of the many food concessions at the fairground. It was all here: waffles, oysters, French fries with ice cream, sausage and peppers, calzones and more. *From* The Newtown Bee.

Another memorable, but unaffiliated, apple pie concession in Dutch Village boasted the pies heated in a beehive oven.

What else was there to eat? Barbecue sandwiches, Belgian waffles, hot dogs, hamburgers, corn on the cob, salt potatoes, popcorn, candy apples, cotton candy, wurst, onion blossoms and pancakes. Yes, pancakes.

"I belonged to the Kiwanis Club in Danbury, and we had a booth outside the big ring of the Big Top, and we sold pancakes," said Phil Bergquist. "Paul Ziegler and I would be in the booth all day and he would holler all day long: *Come get your hot pancakes, just like Mama used to make!*"

Paul, known as the Pancake Mayor, mixed the batter in a dedicated fifty-five-gallon garbage can and stirred it with a boat oar. With a culinary dispenser, they would shoot out an exacting amount of batter onto a grill and serve the thin pancakes with maple syrup and sausage. They served up pancakes for several years until the fair closed.

"Yes, we made money," said Phil. "A couple thousand dollars for the ten days."

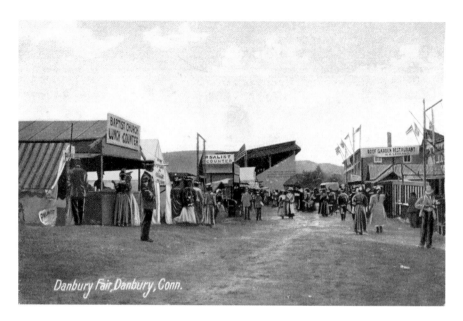

Local churches operated food concessions at the Danbury Fair for half a century. Church Row, as it was later referred to, became part of Goldtown when interest waned in continuing the parish tradition. *Newtown Historical Society.*

CHURCH ROW

Church Row, located just north of the grandstand, was a favorite food destination for fairgoers. Here, Church of Christ, Assumption Church, St. Gregory's and other congregations offered homemade specialties for lunch and dinner.

"The booths were not huge," said Ann Diker, who worked the food booth for her church, St. George. "Each one had its cooking facilities."

The church group did most of the cooking ahead of time at the church and then reheated the few things that were served warm.

"We made kibbe sandwiches, we had hummus and tabbouleh," Ann said. "It was a lot of preparation because of the type of food it is. *Weeks* of work ahead of time."

The meat was prepared, the filling ground and cooked, and then the kibbe could be made. Once it was cooked and cooled off, the church members carted everything over to the fairground and reheated the kibbe before putting it in pita bread. The tabbouleh was also very labor intensive, Ann said.

The women decided to not continue a food concession after two years.

"We couldn't charge enough to make it financially worth it for the church," said Ann, "and it was a tremendous amount of work."

Other churches ceased concessions and the area known as Church Row became part of the new western theme village Goldtown.

Doris Dickinson, born in 1911, recalled her father delivering bread to the concessions on Church Row. In her oral history in *Newtown Remembered*, she explained, "My father, being a baker, furnished bread. Most of the churches had booths where they had food…I remember going with him under the grandstand and leaving off bread.

"After…he would take me to the chance places where they would have the wheel. He would take chances on practically all the numbers in order to give him a very good chance of winning," she said. "I can remember we had Indian blankets; we had pearls, strings of pearls. We had carnival glass, the orange color and the purple color." All treasures from the Danbury Fair.

"The churches would start in July and August and plan what they were going to do," said Paul Trudel. "It brought the community together. You couldn't wait. To get ready, you had to make sure you had the workers, the product/ingredients, the change.

"It wasn't so easy to get change," he noted. "Back in the early '50s all the banks were downtown. So if you were running out of change, you had to send someone all the way downtown to get more change. And people were waiting in line to buy stuff until you got change."

Because the fair closed at seven o'clock—*on the dot!*—in the evenings, concessions started winding down at six thirty. This could be to your benefit if you were hungry and milling about.

"If you were walking by a concession that still had French fries and hamburgers and they were closing and would have to throw them away, they would say, 'You want a hamburger?'" said Paul Trudel. "And they would give it to you."

Bobby Marquis had concessions under the grandstand during Fair Week and on race nights. "There you could buy 'ballpark' foods," said Millie Godfrey.

The other permanent concession stands that dotted the fairground, remained boarded up until the fair rolled around. They would be painted and repaired, of course, during the off-season, just like everything else at the fair.

People who didn't rent buildings brought their own tents or trailers with sides that dropped down and literally staked out their patch of leased fairground.

"Food was *everywhere*," said Alyce Block, who had her first baked potato with broccoli on it at the Danbury Fair.

The fairground was 142 acres, and if you planned your route, you could snack your way right through. Although most of the food concessions were stands, there were a few where you could sit down, such as the Farmer's Daughter, Mary and Joe's Barnyard Inn with eighty seats or Showah's family cafeteria.

"I would come home from working at Showah's and step out of my clothes and into the shower and have that hot water hit me because I couldn't get the smell out of my nose—from the fries and from the grill," remembered Ann Diker, who worked at the restaurant for two years.

Showah's cafeteria was in a big tent, but offered outside seating, too. The longtime fair concession served American food: grilled sausage with peppers and onions, hamburgers, hot dogs and hot apple pie à la mode.

"The apple pie was nice and high and filled with apples," said Ann. "People loved that."

In 1949, the *Spaulding Times* reported that forty hot dog and refreshment concessions at the Danbury Fair served Spaulding products. "One stand, 'Freddies,'" the company newsletter said, "used over a thousand dozen rolls."

An article in the October 9, 1977 *News-Times* reported, "Some estimates put a simple hot dog stand's profit at more than $5,000 during fair week."

Local businesses used food as a springboard to advertise, as evidenced by the Danbury Fair Cook Book they sponsored in 1888. This booklet had advertising on the left side and recipes on the right. The majority of these "useful and reliable recipes" are desserts and tend to include weight instead of dry measurements or measurements in vessels common at the time (teacupful, coffee can). Sometimes, the instructions simply say to add enough flour to make a "stiff batter" or "add a custard," as if every self-respecting cook would know precisely what that meant.

Of course, there were no temperature gauges on stoves at that time, so the heat of the oven is indicated by the terms "quick," "slow" and "hot." On occasion, no size pan or oven temperature is indicated.

Here is a sample of recipes from the Danbury Fair Cook Book.

Tomato Pie: *Take green tomatoes, turn boiling water on them, and let them remain in it a few minutes; then strip off the skin, cut the tomatoes in slices, and put them in deep pie plates. Sprinkle sugar over each layer, and a little ginger. Grated lemon peel and the juice of a lemon improve the pie. Cover the pies with a thick crust, and bake them slowly for about an hour.*

Grape Catsup: *Five pounds grapes boiled and colandered, one and three-quarter pounds of sugar, if sweet grapes, or two pounds, wild, one pint vinegar, one tablespoonful of cinnamon, one tablespoonful of cloves, same of allspice and black pepper, half tablespoonful of salt. Boil until the catsup is a little thick, then bottle and seal.*

Corn Patties: *Eighteen ears of corn grated or cut very fine, add three eggs well beaten, four tablespoonfuls of flour; cook in part butter and part lard (only lard enough to keep butter from burning). Add little salt. Cook on griddle.*

Scollops [sic] *are nice boiled, and then fried, or boiled and pickled, in the same manner as oysters. Take them out of the shells—when boiled, pick out the hearts, and throw the rest away, as the heart is the only part that is healthy to eat. Dip the hearts in flour, and fry them in lard till brown. The hearts are good stewed, with a little water, butter, salt and pepper.*

Ducks *are good stewed like pigeons, or roasted. Two or three onions in the dressing of wild duck takes out the fishy taste they are apt to have. If ducks or any other fowls are slightly injured by being kept too long, dip them in weak saleratus water before cooking them.*

Cocoanut Drops: *One pound of grated cocoanut, three eggs, three-quarters pound of sugar, two tablespoonfuls of flour. To be baked a few minutes in a slow oven. The above quantity will make fifty.*

Custard Tart: *Line a deep plate with a crust; take six or eight apples with the cores taken out, and pared; fill the hole in the apples with preserves; fill the dish with rich custard, and bake half an hour.*

Pound Cake: *One pound of flour, one pound of sugar, one pound of butter, ten eggs, nutmeg. Makes two loaves.*

Cup Cake: *Two cupfuls of sugar, one cupful of sour milk, four eggs, one-half cupful of butter, three cupfuls of flour, one-half teaspoonful of soda.*

7

The Big Top

The Heart of the Fair

*Our folk have had their share of drought and chilling frost but here we are with
food-stuff aplenty, and judging for prizes is going to be most difficult.
—Arlene Yaple, superintendent of the Big Top,*
New York Times, *October 5, 1953*

A new Big Top tent went up in 1951, all 31,000 square feet of canvas. It
sheltered agricultural displays, bands and vendors selling leather purses,
candy, hats, nails, plants, widgets and jewelry in an area 250 feet long by 125
wide behind the administration building.

Bone dry, the tent weighed 7,500 pounds; wet, it weighed thrice that. And
holding it all together was 7,755 feet of rope.

"It was quite a deal getting that tent up," recalls C. Irving Jarvis Jr., son of the
assistant general manager of the fair. "It took at least a couple days by the time
they got it out, sorted it and put it together with roping. The Big Top was put up
in sections—at *least* ten sections—and raised up with blocks and tied off on the
edge of the building. It was a huge tent."

The big tent had a stage for music at one end, and outer ring of 172 concession
booths, and a massive central area dedicated to competitive and inspired farm,
4-H and Grange displays. Many felt it was the heart of the Danbury Fair. Even
though the fair's overall emphasis on agriculture diminished as farms disappeared
from the landscape, the Big Top remained true to its agricultural roots.

"Anyone over three or four years old would love the Big Top," said Millie
Godfrey. And she should know—she first went inside the tent eighty-one
years ago, when *she* was four.

The Big Top tent was thirty-one thousand square feet of canvas sections roped together. Dry, the tent weighed 7,500 pounds. *Danbury Museum and Historical Society Authority.*

The Big Top stage was home to Wendell Cook's band, organ music, tribal dancing, Salad Master demonstrations and square dancing. *From* The Newtown Bee.

"I remember having lunch in the Big Top in the stands there behind the music," she said. Millie and her mother, who had packed their lunch in a shoebox, took the city trolley to the fairground.

"At one time you could walk all the way around the Big Top ring and come out with a whole shopping bag of goodies because they would give away things," said Millie. "A ruler that said 'Danbury Fair' on it. It was good advertisement. The Indians, Princess Goldenrod and her husband were in the Big Top. And, of course all the produce [and] beautiful arrangements of flowers."

ARLENE YAPLE: BIG TOP SUPERINTENDENT

During the last thirty-five years of the fair, Arlene Yaple was Superintendent of the Big Top. She grew up on a farm in New Milford where her family raised champion chickens and collies. Arlene had a long career as a news correspondent for local newspapers and was a ghostwriter. But each year when the fall rolled around, Arlene left her typewriter to take up her command post in the Big Top—a platform with three sides that she called the Goat Pen.

"Arlene 'owned' that Big Top," said Irv Jarvis Jr. "Nothing would go in or out of that Big Top without Arlene's 'OK.' She managed that entire area; she was like a stage manager. She knew all the farmers, knew who was growing something interesting and wanted to introduce that to the public."

Most of Arlene Yaple's official responsibilities were related to the agriculture displays, but she got to know everyone who set up in the Big Top, including all the vendors and entertainers, said Irv.

"If anyone needed something or had a problem, they'd go to Arlene," he said. "She was a great lady and a good organizer. And people listened to her when she said, 'You are going to do this or that.'"

If you didn't listen, Arlene kicked the problem up another level.

"She'd come stomping into the office and say to my father, 'Mr. Jarvis you have to do something about so-and-so. I've told him a dozen times…' And he'd say, 'All right. I'll take care of it.'"

It was the culmination of a year's work finding just the right farmers, Granges and 4-H clubs to create themed displays.

"Arlene was really a down-to-earth person. She was great," said R. Scudder Smith, publisher of *The Newtown Bee* and *Antiques and the Arts Weekly*.

Arlene Yaple was superintendent of the Big Top for the last thirty-five years of the fair. She "ruled" the big tent from a platform she called the Goat Pen. *From* The Newtown Bee.

"She knew *everybody*. She was a great correspondent because she knew what was going on—she didn't miss anything."

Arlene lived in a little ranch house and wrote news for *The Newtown Bee* and other area newspapers. Scudder said when he'd stop by her house she was usually in a robe and big fluffy slippers.

"She was always friendly," said Scudder. "She was just a big happy lady and she *loved* Danbury Fair."

He recalled that she sat on the raised platform acting like Queen Elizabeth.

"She ruled the big tent. You didn't do anything without asking Arlene," said Scudder. "I don't think John Leahy had any say in the Big Top."

FARM DISPLAYS

Fanning out from the center poles of the Big Top were plywood tables filled with fairy tale–sized pumpkins, giant flags made from apples, seed murals, beehives with live colonies, ice harvesting and maple sugaring displays. Farmers from Danbury, Newtown, New Milford, Roxbury and

Fencing of displays became necessary when some fairgoers started to help themselves to an apple or disrupt an exhibit. *From* The Newtown Bee.

places in between would prepare all year to come up with some innovative and fun ways to display that which they grew or used on the farm.

"We raised a lot of vegetables specifically for the Danbury Fair," recalled Eleanor Mayer of Newtown in *Eleanor Mayer's History of Cherry Grove Farm.* "We raised peanuts, for example when Jimmy Carter was in office. We actually grew it in this glass thing. You could look in the glass and see the peanuts growing underneath the bush."

"My father was big on the vegetables," said Eleanor. "He and the agriculture teacher, Vin Gaffney, were partners in the Danbury Fair exhibition every year. In 1926 in a Model T Ford he took pumpkins to the fair. When Mr. Gaffney had a heart attack and died, my father and I carried on for thirty, thirty-five years."

Farmers were paid per table, and there were prizes to be won. It wasn't so much about the money, the farmers said, it was the friendly competition among peers and pride of winning one of the large rosette blue ribbons from the Danbury Fair.

"The Mayers basically won the Big Top every year," recalled Stephen Paproski owner of Castle Hill Farm in Newtown. "They brought all their vegetables, their big pumpkins, their squashes. They were big time. I don't know when they *didn't* win; they were always on the front page of the paper."

150 year old NORTHERN Spy
Apple Tree. IT stood 150
years on Mayer farm, Newtown
CONN. often it Produced
30 Bushel _____ year.

During the last year of the fair, George Mayer and his daughter, Eleanor, exhibited the trunk of a dead Northern Spy apple tree that had grown on the Mayer farm for over 150 years and yielded thirty bushels of apples a year. *From* The Newtown Bee.

George Mayer, a farmer in Newtown, created this prize-winning railroad centerpiece for the Big Top and surrounded it with produce he grew. *From* The Newtown Bee.

Although the Mayers grew special wheats and Hungarian mammoth squash for the fair, they made other types of displays that were quite elaborate.

"One time the theme was 'Railroads' and we made a train out of all types of seed and stuff. It had expression," said Eleanor, who, when interviewed for the book in 2004, claimed she still had that train. "It looked like it was leaning into the wind with smoke coming out. We had a blinker light and we had an electric flasher under the coals so it looked like it was going. We spent so much time on this stuff—just unbelievable."

Another year the Mayers made an exhibit with a motorized mill in water. They gathered rocks from their farmland and moss from the swamps with which to surround the mill.

"The fair wasn't just an October event to us. We started in the fall ordering seeds for the next year. But we worked there like crazy for ten days before the fair growing all kinds of different exhibits for them," Eleanor said. "It had to be done by the Friday before the fair opened. And then we'd just have to come through during the week to clean up and dust it and replace the stuff that wilted."

"The Mayers were next to us every year," recalled Cathy Bronson of Maple Bank Farm in Roxbury. "They always had beautiful tables."

THE GREAT DANBURY STATE FAIR

Cathy's father and uncle operated the farm, then Hurlbut Brothers Farm, when it was primarily a poultry farm with broilers and laying hens. They also grew apples. Lots of apples.

"We grew fifty varieties and our farm did at least two tables of designs with apples for the Danbury Fair," said Cathy. "The tables were four sheets of plywood. When I was young, every inch of the display table had to be covered by apples."

The Hurlbuts recruited friends and neighbors to come polish every apple. And they sought out the person with the best handwriting to make the labels for each variety.

"Everything was measured. And we tried to make the design uniform and sometime we had to change it if we didn't have enough of a particular variety of apple," she said.

"It was a significant part of our activity on the farm and in the family during the year," she said, adding they often grew giant squash and pumpkins for the fair. "Mom and my aunt spent all year designing and preparing for the next year's design."

Cathy's cousin Peter Hurlbut remembered traveling from the farm in Roxbury to set up the display at the Danbury Fair as one of the annual highlights of his childhood.

Apples were polished, labeled and refreshed in displays; later, the viable candidates were made into cider. As many as fifty varieties were in an exhibit. *From* The Newtown Bee.

"That was as good as it got!" said Peter. "It wasn't a time that you would just run to Danbury for amusement; you would go for business. But we certainly got a lot of enjoyment out of what we were doing."

For a few years, the Hurlbuts filled an entire table with apples to create and American "flag"—lighter and darker varieties of apples made the "stripes," grapes made the blue background and the stars were apples cut out with cookie cutters and dipped in paraffin to keep them from turning brown.

Some of their other displays depicted a giant butterfly, a huge flower and an image of King Tut made out of apples, grapes and crabapples. One year,

The clever Hurlbut brothers topped their display of gourds with a Turkish "fellow" wearing a marshmallow fez and smoking a gourd hookah. *From* The Newtown Bee.

they hammered nails all over a large wooden barrel and mounted apples on the nails so the barrel was completely covered. They even dug up an apple tree and some sod from the farm to put on the display table.

"Every day we went to display, and used a feather duster to dust off the tables. The Big Top was a really dusty place!" she said. "We kept a backup supply of apples under tables to replace apples people did take. At some point, chicken wire was put up so people couldn't reach over and disrupt the display."

And what happened to all those apples at the end of the fair? The Hurlbuts brought the apples back home, chose the viable ones, washed them and made full-bodied apple cider.

Earle P. Yaple of New Milford, the superintendent's father, raised pumpkins every year for a Big Top display. In 1957, his exhibit comprised more than five tons of pumpkins and squash. Two years earlier, however, a great mass of the Yaple's annual pumpkin crop was carried away after August hurricanes brought the Great Flood of 1955.

"We salvaged a few," said Arlene that year in a September 25 *New York Times* article. "Some of them may have ended up in Long Island Sound for all we know."

THE GRANGE AND 4-H DISPLAYS

The Grange, formally known as the National Grange of the Order of Patrons of Husbandry, is a nonprofit agricultural fraternity that was founded during the Civil War. The organization advocates for rural America and agriculture and strives to promote faith, hope, charity and fidelity.

Each Grange was provided a ten- by eight-foot table on which to create a display of "the best collective exhibit of farm and garden produce, fruits, flowers, dairy products, culinary articles produced or made by members of the subordinate granges," according to the 1950 fair guide. The Grange members, like the farmers, were competitive, and winners garnered ribbons, trophies and cash prizes.

A 1960 *News-Times* article reports five of the eight counties in Connecticut, as well as fourteen towns, were represented in the Granges' fruit and vegetables displays in the Big Top. The towns were Roxbury, Newtown, Redding, Cornwall, Brookfield, Shelton, New Milford, Monroe, Torrington, Ridgefield, Southington, Danbury, Middletown and Winchester.

The Redding Grange still exhibits a cabinet full of trophies and ribbons won at the Danbury Fair. This display garnered one of those ribbons. *From* The Newtown Bee.

Superintendent Arlene Yaple provided the themes for the displays until later years, when she asked the Granges to collectively choose one. In 1976, the Redding Grange display reflected that year's theme: From the Kitchen Comes Goodness for Both Body and Mind.

"One year someone brought a little pot-bellied stove, and we made our display into a living room scene, just like a home," said Marie Parker of the Redding Grange. "We'd always have homemade canning, homemade breads, cakes, pies—you name it."

In the Big Top, these were just a component of the overall display, as were the apples, squash, mums, other flowers and vegetables that were often included in their exhibits. The Redding Grange boasts a cabinet full of ribbons and trophies as testament to the success of their efforts.

"Everything had to be 'just so' or you would get marked down by the judges," recalled Joan Ziegler, longtime Redding Grange member. "Some years they gave us a theme; in later years, we had to think of our own themes. We worked as a committee to create a display that would show people what the Grange was and to get more members."

Joan well remembers the superintendent of the Big Top.

"Arlene Yaple would not let you take anything out of that exhibit until *exactly* seven o'clock on the last day," said Joan. "Our Grange always had a meeting that night, and we were always late because we had to wait to break down the exhibit."

4-H is a nationwide program of the Cooperative Extension Service of land-grant universities with the mission to help youth develop by focusing on the four "H"s: head, heart, hands and health. Although most people associate 4-H participation in fairs with raising and showing animals, clubs had their own section of the Big Top where they displayed projects.

The types of exhibits 4-H would have at the fair would be birdhouses or little animal cages made by youth in its membership. They, too, vied for prizes.

"The role of the Big Top has changed from competition to education," said Arlene Yaple in an October 2, 1981 article in the *New York Times*. "It used to be entirely competition. People used to get really excited to see the competition between farms. But the people are really interested in learning now, too."

"The Big Tent was fabulous for learning about agriculture," said Alyce Block, who created the Traveling Farm Agricultural Education Program and presented it to thirty-five thousand children in Fairfield County schools.

BIG TOP STAGE

Whereas Arlene Yaple was responsible for arranging the exhibitors in the Big Top, C. Irving Jarvis Sr. was the one who booked the concessionaires as well as the entertainment.

"My dad would book the bands, the stage shows, the entertainment that was there, such as Princess Goldenrod and Indian dancing," said Irv Jarvis Jr. "[He booked] everything under the sun entertainment-wise that was there."

The Big Top Stage performers were as varied as those who set up concessions and exhibits under the tent. "Tudo" Tangua played fiddle while Bob or Al Brundage called square dancing sets on the stage. Wendell Cook Circus Show Band regularly performed here, as did Victor Zembruski's polka band; these two bands also performed in the parade or grandstand show and are profiled in the chapter on entertainment. Vendors occasionally rated billing on the Big Top schedule of events with such offerings as the Saladmaster Cooking Demonstration.

Virginia Wren, longtime talk-show host for WLAD, became known as the "Voice of the Danbury Fair" with her regular broadcasts from the Big Top.

Local talent, such as organist Emile Buzaid, was also highlighted on stage. Even schoolkids were invited to perform under the tent.

"When I was in eighth grade in Hayestown School," said JoAnn Schofield, "our Glee Club wrote a song about the Danbury Fair and sang it in the big tent, on the stage, over the radio. We were in our robes. It was exciting. Mr. Leahy was still alive then."

"I belonged to Brundage's; we demonstrated square dancing on the Big Top stage," said Dorothy Pribulo of Danbury. "Mostly country music, and all the different dances. You swing your partner. The more I swung, the more I loved it!"

Square dancing and the country music that accompanied it were popular features at the fair for years.

"I was a square dancer because that was what we did in my day!" Dorothy laughed. "We wore the swinging skirts and the tops. There wasn't much to do during the war; so we looked forward to dancing and traveled all over the area to dance."

8

Concessionaires

Wares, Rides and Midway Games

Before you can get a boy to tote a bucket of water or turn a grindstone,
you can get this knife sharp!
—knife-sharpener hawker

I still remember it. His inflection. He had a *way* of saying it," said Garry Burdick, recalling how fascinated he was by the pitch of the knife-sharpener salesman. "To me, that was poetry of some kind. The way he presented it. He did it over and over all those years."

Garry and his childhood friend Stuart rode their bikes from Redding to the Danbury Fair, ditched them in the woods and snuck into the fair by climbing the fence (two fences after Leahy caught on). The two chums looked at everything but particularly enjoyed the hawkers.

"There was the guy who sold car polish," Garry said. "He always had a nice car. He'd polish the hood of the car and put lighter fluid on it and hit it with a match. *Phooom!* That was another fellow to listen to."

Who were these people who came to the Danbury Fair, year after year, to pitch their wares?

Some were local business owners who wanted a presence at the fair. Some were craftsmen. Others were salesmen for corporations. Or just fellows like the knife-sharpener salesman who followed the fair circuit with his product in tow.

"A lot of people saved their vacation time for fair week so they could open up a booth and make money for those ten days," said lifelong Danbury resident Millie Godfrey. "It was a big boost for Danbury and big boost for

Farmers and cowboys alike wanted to see the latest that John Deere, McCormick and Farmall had to offer for manure spreaders, tractors, hay balers and milking machines. *Photograph by Garry Camp Burdick.*

the Danburites. People from out of town who had concessions would rent rooms around town in homes."

Concessionaires sold small items like mops, cigarettes, candy, cleaning products, wooden toys, hats, jewelry, plants and flowers and everything else under the sun. Larger items included stoves, chainsaws, remote-controlled lawn mowers, refrigerators, convertible beds and the latest in farm equipment.

"John Deere, McCormick, Farmall—the different companies that were out there in those days would all bring their wares to the fair," said Alyce Block of Monroe, a longtime board member and committee chair for Farm Bureau. "Manure spreaders, tractors, hay balers, milking machines and logging equipment for people who did forestry. The farmers really liked to go see all that new stuff."

Alyce said her late husband, Burton Block, who had a livestock and wholesale meat business, might not necessarily buy right on the spot but soon after would make a purchase based on what he saw at the fair. Yet Alyce and Burt both loved the Big Top.

"The main reason Burt went to the fair was all the animals, but he *loved* the big tent because he was somebody who wanted the new stuff, the new way to chop your onions, the new way to wash your floor—he loved all that stuff," said Alyce. "And we'd come home with it all. I'd always have a new cucumber slicer. The kids all had leather pocket books that were hand-tooled. We had everything from the fair."

Vendors had eleven areas from which to choose a spot to set up shop. Returning concessionaires had until March 1 of the following year to secure their same location for the next year's fair; after that date, it was fair game for newcomers.

"Before the fair was over, a lot of them had a habit of coming into my dad's office and saying, 'Here's a down payment for next year; I want the same spot,'" said C. Irving Jarvis Jr. "So the fair was being booked before it ended."

The enormous Big Top Circle and Bazaar alone boasted 172 booths for concessionaires, each approximately ten by ten feet. In 1961, spaces were offered for eighty dollars, with a twenty-five-dollar premium for the more desirable corner locations. These booths ringed the big top tent with two wide aisles—the Building Circle and Big Top Circle—separating them. The center of the enormous Big Top was always reserved for displays of fruit, grain, vegetables, flowers and plants, as well as the Big Top Arena bandstand and bleachers.

"I worked in the Big Top and sold the English lavender and the balsam fir incense with the little cabin," said JoAnn Schofield, who worked for ten years

The Big Top was the place to shop for jewelry, flowers, leather bags, taffy, mops and handmade wooden toys. *Photograph by Garry Camp Burdick.*

at the fair for different local businesses, including Bonnadio Candy. "They had potpourris, too. I'd smell like all of that for weeks afterward!"

JoAnn's sister worked with her at concessions, and they always had a lot of fun. One year, when their booth was next to the Stetson Hat Company's table, they noticed something fishy going on.

"There was a group of people who were handing hats down, stealing hats, and we caught them," she said. "My sister and I were both given beautiful hats from the Stetson Hat Company for catching them."

"Princess Goldenrod and her husband came every year as long as I can remember," said eighty-five-year-old Millie Godfrey. "They wore Indian garb, sold trinkets, and they were in the parade every day."

Millie's father had a private museum in Danbury with sixty thousand Indian artifacts, and through this shared interest in Native American culture, she became acquainted with the couple.

Another concessionaire made Great Danbury Fair Saltwater Taffy right there under the big tent and sold it in a box with a picture of the fair on its top. And many local florists, including Melillo Florists, Cleary's, Judd's Flower Shop and Zinser's Florists, sold cut flowers and plants.

"My favorite was the Big Top," recalled Marietta Bailey, "because Zinser's Florist always displayed the big dahlias. Oh! They were so beautiful. To this day we raise dahlias in our garden every year."

"You could get a lot of freebies in the Big Top," said Paul Trudel. "You never bought a yardstick; the paint store, like Nero's, would give you a yardstick. You'd go back the next year, and they'd give you another yardstick. Meeker's Hardware would have a stand there with all their nails and screws. They all gave you samples."

In addition to the Big Top, the fairground had four large, rectangular permanent buildings for concessionaires. Colonial Hall had thirty-three rentals, each ten by eight feet and costing seventy dollars with a five-dollar premium for a corner booth. Machinery Hall held twenty-nine booths, each twelve and half by twelve and half feet and rented for fifty-five dollars, and the Home Show offered thirty-two twelve-and-a-half- by ten-foot spaces for fifty-five dollars.

Country Hall was different from the other three "sister" buildings in that it had no center row of vendor space; also, one end of this building permanently housed the Barnum Show, a tribute to John Leahy's idol P.T. Barnum.

Ben Speglevin, a Danbury merchant, sold Silver King canister-style vacuum cleaners in a booth at Country Hall for twenty-five years until the fair closed. His booth was one of thirty-nine in the building, a twelve-and-a-half- by fourteen-and-a-half-foot space that was rented for sixty-five dollars in the early 1960s.

"He loved it," said his daughter Jill Austin, now owner of Ben's Vacuum Mart in Danbury. "My father was charismatic and charming. He sometimes said: 'It walks, it talks, it crawls on its belly like a reptile,' just to get people to laugh."

Jill and her five siblings would load the family station wagon with tables, machines, lighting, curtains, signs and floorings—everything their father needed to create his display.

The floor of Country Hall was concrete, so Ben laid out an area rug and a piece of linoleum on which to demonstrate his wares. His booth, like the others in the building, had three sides for privacy, but the merchants got to know one another and chatted to pass the time during slow periods. They also minded one another's stores when someone needed a break.

Vendors, like Ben Speglevin, who sold Silver King vacuums, could rent a space in the Big Top, Colonial Hall, Machinery Hall, Home Show, Country Hall or seven other areas in the 142-acre fairground. *Jill Austin.*

The high-end stainless steel vacuums, which sold for between $250 and $300 in the late 1950s, were marketed for household use even though they were commercial grade.

"As people walked by, my dad would catch them looking, and he'd turn the machine on," said Jill. "He'd have a tin of nuts and bolts, and he'd throw some down on the floor, and he'd suck them up—*thunk, thunk* into the tank."

When he had their attention, Ben Speglevin would go into his sales presentation, add the squeegee tool and demonstrate the Silver King's innovative wet-vac feature. He kept only a few vacuums at the booth because he knew no one wanted to tote a big box around the fairground.

"Generally people would buy them and pick them up at the store," said Jill. "The fair really helped generate a lot of business for his store in selling vacuums. It really was a good base because people came from New York City and from all over Connecticut."

Six other locations where vendors could set up shop were Goldtown, Village Museum, New Amsterdam Village, Shopping Center, New England Village and outside space on nine midways where merchants were charged nine dollars per frontage foot.

In 1961, Garry Burdick, who, as a child, had been so fascinated by the fair vendors, rented a booth himself. He came from a family of hatters but found the lure of a new college major—photography—too enticing to follow in his forefather's footsteps. He became a freelance photographer and decided he might try offering portraits for two dollars at the Danbury Fair.

He set up his studio in New England Village in a little old house with a peaked roof, a door and windows on each side. He paid ninety dollars to rent the space for the nine days of the fair, plus ten dollars to add electrical service.

"The house was right about at the center of there looking outward, so it was a great spot," said Garry. "I had signs: Ye Olde Photographer. I had a beard and wore a big white coat."

He had hats in his studio for people to wear. And to add to the "romance" of his offering, Garry used the little-known process of making paper negatives.

"The idea is to focus an image on the paper," he said. He used a big camera that accommodated an eight- by ten-inch paper holder. He'd squeeze a bulb that opened the lens shutter and count to three or four.

"It was a long exposure; they had to sit very still," he said. Some children did move, but Garry never took a second shot because his overhead was so high.

Fairgoers who were willing to take the time to pose, could leave with a caricature, silhouette, fine art or photographic portrait as a keepsake. *From* The Newtown Bee.

Garry took the exposed sheets home every night, developed and dried them. In the darkroom, he then laid another sheet of photographic paper on top of his paper negative and put the "sandwich" on a light table to expose the fresh sheet. This created a positive image he developed and faithfully mailed out the next day to his fair customers.

"I sold one hundred pictures for the nine days, an average of ten a day," said Garry. "I was hoping for twenty or thirty a day at least."

One day, the photographer dropped his price to one dollar per portrait but that didn't help.

"I was right next to somebody who made fudge. The guy made a fortune," Garry shook his head and laughed. "He had people lined up. They came for fudge. They didn't come to have their picture taken."

If they didn't want their photograph taken, fairgoers could have their caricature drawn or a formal portrait.

In 1967, Carl J. Tomanio sold Pebble Candy in Goldtown, right outside the Big Top area. He had seen this unusual treat on a recent trip and decided to order a few cases from a company in Ohio to sell at the Danbury Fair.

"If you saw the candy in a dish, you would not pick one up because you would think they were small stones," said Carl, who painted tall signs with a cartoon character to attract customers. "The stones were all different shapes."

Many of the hundreds of concessions, such as this Pebble Candy stand, were operated by local people who took vacation time to work during Fair Week. *Photograph by Carl Tomanio.*

Carl ran the booth with his wife and his father. They had paid $1.50 per box and sold them for double the price. They gave away free samples to entice people to buy.

"People were in a spending mood. They wanted to go home with something," he said.

The pebble candy was beautifully packaged in boxes, and the Tomanios sold their entire stock. Although it wasn't profitable when he considers expenses, Carl did enjoy the perks of being a vendor that year.

"As concessionaires, we could go into the fairgrounds any time, before anything was going on," he said. "So I'd take my car and go around the racetrack!"

THE GREAT DANBURY STATE FAIR

Newspaper accounts of the day reveal vendors were reticent to talk about just how much they made during the ten-day fair. Perhaps they were afraid one of the dozen employees of the Connecticut Tax Department assigned to the Danbury Fair might read about their profits.

A list of concessionaires was provided to the tax specialists by fair management. It was their job to ensure the state got its due in sales tax. At the time, hot dog stands and others did not charge tax on sales less than one dollar.

In 1977, the *News-Times* reported vendors had an aggregate sales tax of $20,000 to $25,000, which translates to a collective gross income for concessionaires of $285,000 to $357,000. Today, that value would equal $1.4 million.

THE MIDWAY GAMES AND RIDES

"No matter which game you try, you lose," warned an unidentified 1894 news article about the Danbury Fair.

That is probably one of the few things that most people would say never changed about the fair.

Everywhere you looked, John Leahy had tucked one of his one thousand figures to delight visitors—pixies, reindeer, giant raccoons, pirates and storybook characters. *From* The Newtown Bee.

"The carnies, the people who were running the games, you may as well just give them your money because there was no way you were going to win," said Brenda McKinley, who was in high school when the Danbury Fair closed. "They were pretty much out to take your money. We knew that; we never played the games."

Other kids would try, Brenda said, especially one game that required you to drop five disks and cover the image of a circle.

"The guy would say, 'It's *easy*,'" she recalled. "He'd show you—he'd drop the disks and cover the circle. You'd drop the disks and there was always something showing. I never saw anyone win that."

At least the rides at the Danbury Fair offered visitors the opportunity to walk away with something—a fun memory.

Danburite Jill Austin remembered riding on camels and elephants with her sister at the Danbury Fair.

"They had a seat and bars on the side for safety," she said. "They'd take you around a little area but you thought it was miles. It was probably only five minutes, but back then, it seemed like some safari."

Children who rushed to the midway would find their favorites waiting for them—the Ferris wheel, the rollercoaster, the flying swings—as well as some new thrills in the Zipper, Sky Wheel, Tilt-a-Whirl and Sky Diver.

Although the Danbury Fair had its share of rides, most people remember it for the enormous Big Top, races, ox pulls, theme villages and amazing array of food. *From* The Newtown Bee.

"My high school friend's father would give us a whole roll of tickets every year," said Danbury native Ann Diker, "and we would ride the swings and Octopus until we couldn't stand up straight anymore."

The Danbury Fair owned some rides during the first two decades John Leahy was manager. A serendipitous conversation between Leahy and one of his food concessionaires created opportunity for both businessmen that ensued until the manager's death and subsequent closing of the fair.

Robert Marquis, a woodworker by trade, operated seven hot dog stands at the fair, as well as a restaurant concession beneath the grandstand that was also open every Saturday night during the summer race season.

In the mid-1960s, John Leahy asked if he wanted to buy the thirty-foot slide that was falling into disrepair. Bobby bought the slide, spent a great deal of time and money to repair it and then brought it back to the fair as his own attraction.

This transaction sparked Bobby's interest in owning more amusement rides. After a few years of nerve-racking debt and inspired business decisions, the entrepreneur had settled into a very profitable business, Marquis Amusement Co., Inc.

Bobby was known as a stickler for maintaining his rides; they were always spotless and mechanically sound. Unlike other concessionaires' rides, if a light bulb went out on a Marquis amusement, it was immediately replaced. His employees wore blue slacks and light blue shirts with his company's logo.

Soon, his reputation spread, and he developed a regular circuit but always in the region.

Not only did Bobby Marquis eventually own and operate most of the rides at the Danbury Fair, but also he offered corporate picnic packages that included rides and food. In 1978, he began to lease the Danbury Fairground during the summer so corporations that didn't have the property could still enjoy a Marquis picnic.

"We always thought it was a shame the fair only lasted ten days and people couldn't enjoy it all year-round," said Millie Godfrey. "Eventually, they had corporate picnics in summer time. Craft shows in summer time."

But that was after John W. Leahy died. And many people believed it was too late to turn the tide of development.

9

Now *That's* Entertainment

Country Music, Hell Drivers and Dancing Bears

The cigar smokers' ring-blowing contest, billed in the Connecticut tobacco industry's promotion as "the first such contest in the United States,"…will be judged on the number of rings, firmness of the rings, and their size.
—New York Times, *September 19, 1954*

With twelve dedicated performance areas, the Danbury Fair was a whirling-dervish of entertainment. Hot dog–eating chimpanzees, Wild West shows, Indian dancing, ventriloquists, smoke ring–blowing contests, Hell Drivers, comedy acts, Chinese aerialists, ostrich races and music were in every corner of the 142-acre fairground.

"You could *hear* the fair as you approached," said Danbury resident Carl Tomanio. "It was all so exciting!"

During the early years, the fair offered musical entertainment in the evening. A lighthearted mix of dance, song and comedy followed when vaudeville acts became popular. Then for many years, the fair closed at dusk, a tradition John Leahy followed by closing the fairground at the specified time, 6:00 or 6:30 p.m. in the 1950s and then, in later years, promptly at 7:00 p.m.

The fair ran for six and then nine days so that it spanned two weekends, and finally it was expanded to ten days to include Columbus Day.

Each day was so packed with entertainment and fun that it was impossible to see it all in one visit. The animal circus performance alone lasted an hour and forty minutes.

Grandstand shows included zany events, such as ostrich races and the challenge of the most number of people from the audience to climb an elephant. *From* The Newtown Bee.

Fairgoers who had been attending for years often came with a plan. They knew what they wanted to see and how to approach the myriad events on the schedule each day.

"We would do the big walk around," said Brenda McKinley, thinking back to the strategy she and her friends had during the late seventies. "We'd do the perimeter. We'd make sure we'd see everything."

"I loved Zembruski's polka music and the dancing and all," said Hilda Nichols. "That was the first thing I'd want to see. Victor played the accordion and his wife, Sophie, sang."

Performances of all types were primarily held in these venues:

- Big Top Stage
- Motor Mall Arena
- Goldtown Music Hall
- Theater in New England Village
- Bandstand in Dutch Village
- Orange Bowl Stadium
- World of Mirth Theater
- Bandstand in the Main Plaza
- Santa Fe Stage
- Yankee Stadium

- Blue Ribbon Stadium
- Main Grandstand

"A lot of the fairs built around the stars," said C. Irving Jarvis Jr., a retired New York City television producer. In the 1950s and '60s, he tried to convince his father, the assistant general manager of the Danbury Fair, to use his contacts to locate big-name entertainers.

"Dad and Leahy just didn't want the big acts," said Irv.

"It wasn't the money—they spent a LOT of money on the circus acts. They had people come in from all over the world—aerial acts, very expensive acts," he said. "They didn't want Sinatra and the rest of them. They didn't think it fit."

Jarvis and Leahy also chose not to offer video or other contemporary games.

"They wanted to keep it a country fair," said Irv. "That was really the reason why the Danbury Fair didn't become as modern as some of the fairs."

Fairgoers loved to watch and participate in the myriad competitions at the fair—smoke-ring blowing, axe throwing, boat races, hippopotamus challenges and so much more. *Photograph by Robert Mannion. Danbury Museum and Historical Society Authority.*

Slogans used in promotion of the fair reflect this "down country" depiction: "Hi! Ho! Come to the Fair!" and the "Happiest Fairground."

Although there was always something "NEW!" at the fair, many exhibitors, concessionaires and entertainers returned year after year. Even the professionals looked forward to the Danbury Fair; it was such a great venue and people became friendly with one another.

"Many performers followed a fair circuit; some started in Florida and worked their way up the coast," said Irv. "That's why Dad and Leahy had their fair after the Springfield Exhibition. The Danbury Fair was the end of the line, the last big fair for most of the acts and concessionaires."

THE MUSICIANS

When Goldtown was built, country western music naturally followed. Headliners included Carolyn Chase, who played at the fair for twenty years, yodeler Ginger Mae, Smokey Warren and Dottie Mae, Stella and Company, Marian King, Orange Blossom Special and Cowboy Billy Smith.

In Dutch Village, fairgoers would hear German music by Papa Bear Band or Ted DiGeorgia. At the Motor Mall Arena, Fly By Night String Band would play bluegrass and folk.

Polka music was incredibly popular at the fair. Victor Zembruski of Naugatuck and his orchestra played throughout the day in the Main Bandstand. When the daily parade began, Zembruski's Orchestra grew wheels and rolled through the crowd alongside the elephants, clowns and Clydesdales.

Known as the Polka King of Connecticut, Victor Zembruski recorded two hundred songs and was so popular in the region that he would attract as many as two thousand people to an event. In the 1969 issue of the *Danbury Fair News*, he was billed as a "Danbury Fair Tradition."

"They had a particular sound to their music," said Paul Trudel of Danbury. "If you heard it, you knew it was them playing."

The Zembruskis hosted what is likely the longest-running radio show in America, a Sunday morning show on WATR Radio 1320 AM featuring Polish music. Victor started the program in 1934 when he was twenty-two; his wife, Sophie, joined him and continued the show after his death until 2008, when she retired at ninety years old. It was first called *Polka Time*, then *The Polish Eagle Show* and finally *The Sophie Zembruski Show*. Their daughter, Laurie Hoxey, continues to host the show.

Right: Goldtown was home to country music artists Carolyn Chase and the Triple A Ranch Gang (on stage here), Cowboy Billy Smith, Ginger Mae and Stella and Company. *Photograph by Garry Camp Burdick.*

Below: The King of Polka, Victor Zembruski, became a Danbury Fair "tradition." *From left, clockwise*: Stanley Barclay, Victor Zembruski on drums, Henry Zembruski, Walter Lesinak and Joe Steponitis. *Photograph by C. Korker. Danbury Museum and Historical Society Authority.*

Governor McConnaughy dances with Lois Mackay on the Big Top stage as "Tudo" Tangua fiddles and Al Brundage calls. Bleachers under the tent held two hundred. *State Archives, Connecticut State Library.*

Victor's brother, Felix, was at one time part of Victor's orchestra but then went his own way. Felix also performed at the Danbury Fair under his own billing: the Prince of Polka.

Al Brundage and the Danbury Fair Cornhuskers gave visitors an earful of fiddling music and an eyeful of square dancing. They performed on the Big Top Stage, which had bleacher seating for a few hundred.

Tons of Fun, a group of women who sang and danced in Goldtown, was an act that made light of being heavy. Each performer had to maintain a weight of over two hundred pounds but be "agile enough" to dance her way through two shows a day. More than the group's singing and dancing, fairgoers were attracted to its costuming (think: abundance of flesh in fishnet stockings and Indy 500 checkered-flag outfits that look like skirted bathing suits) and self-derisive lines. This one appeared in the October 6, 1977 *News-Times*: "Our curves may be dangerous but they cannot be avoided."

Seven women established the act in 1968, but within ten years, they were a mere trio. Fewer numbers didn't stop them from inviting men up on stage for a dance contest whereby one or more recruits were "sent flying" to the far end of the stage by some hip action of a hefty performer.

Music Inspired by the Danbury Fair

"The Danbury Fair Polka" was written in 1968 by John Carvette of the Carvette School of Music in Danbury, with lyrics by Carvette and Dana Willson Briggs. The song, which mentions Leahy and his assistant general manager, C. Irving Jarvis, by name, was dedicated to John W. Leahy.

Other songs that appeared in sheet music were "The Danbury Fair" by Lindsay McPhail and Walt Michels and "The Danbury Fair for Me" by Robert Stagg. The latter has a copyright of 1908 and, at that time, had the honor of being the "official song" of the Danbury Fair.

Composer Charles Ives grew up in Danbury and was so smitten by the fair in his hometown, he wrote "Skit for Danbury Fair" at the turn of the century.

Dave King, a contemporary singer and songwriter of acoustic rock, said he is best known for his works that "celebrate the glory days of Danbury," which include a song and music video about the fair and a song about the Racearena.

"'The Danbury Fair' song is the piece of music/recording that's given me the most notoriety," said Dave. "It moves me that people have that kind of reaction—that's really cool."

In September 2012, the Connecticut General Assembly honored Dave with an official citation commending him for his artistic contributions in support of the history of the city.

Grandstand Shows

The grandstand show was free on weekdays but had a separate admission on weekends. In 1977, general admission to the fair was $2.50 for adults and $1.50 for children; the weekend grandstand show price was an additional $2 for adults and $0.99 for children. Nobody seemed to mind the extra charge.

"The *talent* that came there!" said Danburite Carl Tomanio. "Trapese artists. Joie Chitwood and his stunt drivers—cars going through a fire barrier, cars driving on two wheels. Some things we had never seen."

Daredevil auto stunt shows were featured throughout the years: a series of "Hell Drivers" (Lucky Teter's, Jack Kochman's, R.C. Connally's and "Irish" Horan's) and finally Joie Chitwood's Thrill Show. Fairgoers were kept on the edges of their Grandstand seats as cars flew off ramps and defied gravity for one hundred feet until meeting another ramp, did Roman steeple chases and flipped end over end.

"Joie Chitwood put on a great show," said Irv. "He ran at Indianapolis. A number of years after Lucky Teter got killed, Joie Chitwood decided to start a thrill show. He had a lot of guys who worked in the motion picture industry, crashing cars and jumping out of planes."

Joie Chitwood Jr. took over the show. And then his son continued it on the West Coast, said Irv.

Chitwood started in Florida and ended the season at the Danbury Fair. Chevrolet was his sponsor for many years, providing him with the newest models in white at the start of the each run. Joie Chitwood is rumored to have been able to drive a car on two wheels for five miles. When he did a similar stunt for the grandstand show, the audience would see the word *Chevrolet* painted underneath his car.

"Joie Chitwood used to have a billboard that said: 'This is the last show—we gotta do something with these cars so we're going to crack them up for you!'" said Irv Jarvis.

Other grandstand shows featured an Indian who rode a motorcycle around the inside of a large "barrel," Chinese aerialists, Royal Canadian Mounted Police, bears who wore tutus and balanced on beach balls and Lipizzan Stallions of Austria.

Carl Tomanio remembered a grandstand show where a man climbed twenty feet and jumped—with his cape fluttering behind him—into four feet of water.

Until his death in 1969, C. Irving Jarvis booked them all. Then Fred Fearn became assistant general manager and assumed that responsibility.

"They had everything—circus acts from time to time, aerial acts, animals, elephants—you name it," said Irv Jr.

Wendell Cook Circus Show Band played background music for most of the grandstand shows.

"I was there all the time, so I was familiar with the type of music he'd play for the elephant acts, the trapeze acts and the sway-bar acts," recalled Irv.

Animal acts were always a favorite with fairgoers, whether the elegant Lipizzan Stallions or dancing bears in overalls and skirts. *Danbury Museum and Historical Society Authority.*

"He had music for all that stuff. He played all over the world. That's all he did, play circus music. For years and years."

Gene Holter's Movieland Animals of Hollywood, California, was another favorite show. The company trained animals for films and toured the country. Irv explained they came as a "complete package"—the animals were on display with elephant rides offered throughout Fair Week, they were in the parade and the enterprise offered professional acts as well as audience acts for the grandstand show.

"They had a guy who wrestled the tiger and a 'sleeping' cowboy whose horse would push him and pull his covers off," said Irv. "They'd call people down from the audience: 'Let's see if we could get fifty people on the hippopotamus!' Wendell Cook would play music and they would try to get on this hippo and try to ride it around the infield."

Some of the zaniest events were the ostrich races. Volunteers from the audience rode in little carts behind the birds and used brooms to steer.

Gene Holter's Movieland Animals and their stunts enthralled spectators. The company trained animals for use in movies. *Photograph by Robert Mannion. Danbury Museum and Historical Society Authority.*

"The only way they could get the ostrich to turn left or right was to make them 'blind' in one eye," recalled Irv Jarvis. "So to get them to turn left you'd cover up the right eye with the broom but it didn't always work. They were funny. And they could move!"

When he was a boy in 4-H, Stephen Paproski helped walk the ostriches in the parade on the days when his own animal was not on the schedule.

"Sometimes there would be four of us holding an ostrich down. They had harnesses on, and we'd be holding on both sides," said Stephen. "They're big, and when they want to go, they want to *go*."

"Ostriches are fast runners; lickety-split they go around that track," said Alyce Block, who witnessed an accident during one of the shows. "Somehow the cart tipped over and the ostrich fell. It got up and was dragging the man and the cart around. Then the ambulance came."

"I would never *ever* recommend anybody ride an ostrich!" said Alyce, laughing.

Opposite, bottom: Audience participation was part of the fun in the grandstand show. Here volunteers try to steer ostriches down the racetrack with brooms. *Photograph by Robert Mannion. Danbury Museum and Historical Society Authority.*

10

Livestock, Petting Zoo and Parade

You just don't drag your cow out of the barn and take it up there and show it.
It's a devotion: training it to behave, to walk on a lead rope and to do certain jobs
that are required.
—*Alyce Block, board member and committee chair of the Farm Bureau*

Whereas the Big Top was the center for learning about agriculture, the animal barns lining the fairground at Backus Avenue and Farm Road were where visitors would find unusual breeds as well as fine specimens of common livestock.

Breed and showmanship competitions were a highlight for farmers. They would walk through the barns, checking out one another's chickens, while city dwellers might have their first glimpse of a heifer. Children loved the small animal barns. If they wanted to touch and feed animals, they would make a beeline over to the Petting Zoo near the grandstand.

"I loved going to the petting zoo," said Ron Gunther. "You were actually in with the goats. If you had food, they'd be jumping up on you. If you turned your back on them, you'd get butt in the behind."

The dedicated barns on the fairground housed ponies, goats, sheep, show dogs, percherons, show horses, swine, poultry and game birds, cattle, oxen and elephants. Rhesus monkeys were in the more centralized "Monkey House."

"Inside the barns you never saw so many different rabbits in your life," said Alyce Block. "Some with big long hair, some with big long ears, every color rabbit, and some were *huge*."

The perimeter of the fairground had barns for horses, ponies, swine, chickens, ducks, cattle and elephants. In later years, the fair had more livestock exhibition than competition. *From* The Newtown Bee.

Jesse Snow was a regular exhibitor at the Danbury Fair. In 1949, he exhibited 1,500 chickens of 100 varieties, including an Australian Kiwi. In a *New York Times* article of October 3, the poultry farmer explained the Kiwi is "the only chicken in the land that has silken feathers."

In the Poultry Barn, each chicken had its history displayed on its cage.

"The histories would include the breed, the farm that they were from, maybe the ages," said Alyce Block. "If they were prize egg layers, it might have production history—how many eggs."

Garnering awards at fairs could potentially increase the value of an animal for a farmer, especially if he was interested in siring it.

"A bull's history might include the cows it sired and the production of how many pounds of milk came from each cow they sired and what they produced as far as how many calves that came down the line that carried that sire's name," said Alyce. "There were a lot of really good genes in our area. The very famous Ivanhoe bull, which came out of Kellogg Farm in Derby, had bloodlines all over; it was the most famous bull in this area."

JUDGING BREED AND SHOWMANSHIP

"The judging was always a highlight to the farmers and 4-H kids," said Alyce. Her late husband, Burton Block, had a livestock and wholesale meat business for six decades in Monroe

Although her husband had no time to raise animals for show, he just loved being a spectator for the showmanship and breed contests at the Danbury Fair.

"Burt was very good at judging—it was his business," said Alyce. "He'd look to the udder, he'd look to the chest, the straightness of the back, to the rump. Of course he was a meat man, too. There are certain ways you look at a dairy cow and certain ways you look at a beef animal.

"And he'd always point all this stuff out to me," she said. "He'd say: Look—see the udders? They all hang even; they all hang straight. That one there, she's a three-titter. Uh! Nope. Won't win."

While watching the judges do the first pull of prize candidates, Burt would often tell Alyce he thought the award order should be different, that number three belonged where two was and so forth.

"First thing you know, the judge would walk back over and switch them around, almost as if he'd heard Burt," Alyce laughed. "It happened many, many times. It was his life. It was his business."

She remembered how touching it was to see a 4-H youth with a pillow and blanket sleeping right next to his cow, bull or calf in the barns.

"Those people were so dedicated—they scrubbed their animals, scrubbed their hooves and polished them and brushed the tails on the cows," recalled Alyce. "Those animals were so clean and the bedding, too."

Training was the key element for showing at the fair. The other entrants would not tolerate a cow in a neighboring stanchion bellowing all day long, she said, nor did the fair management abide an animal that kicked when people passed by.

Stephen Paproski, a third-generation dairy farmer and owner of Castle Hill Farm in Newtown, was about twelve years old when he joined the Twisting Hillbillies 4-H Club. A year later, he was standing in front of the grandstand at the Danbury Fair as Grand Champion for the 4-H Breed Class.

"Each breed champion got to walk in the parade," Stephen recalled. "Leahy called me up and handed me a trophy and the big blue rosette they would give out. I was so honored."

When Stephen joined 4-H, most of the kids in his group were children of dairy farmers in Monroe, Trumbull, Nichols and Newtown. They met at Fairfield Hills State Hospital in Newtown, where their leader, Don Anderson, was herdsman.

"My father and grandfather raised animals here. I picked a couple out, and we worked with them," he said. "You should start months and months and months ahead of time but I was always working and fooling around with my friends, so we didn't really start until a couple weeks before the fair."

But a cow is not easily trained, he said.

"You put a rope on a cow, and they just stand there; you can't pull them," Stephen said. "Sometimes you tie them to a tree and let them get used to the rope. Little by little you work with them."

Stephen and his other 4-H friends who entered the contest at the fair were allowed to sleep in a ten- by ten-foot shed with a heater—a spot usually reserved for owners of oxen. The youth were a little rambunctious, and Danbury Fair security decided to send them a message by locking them in the shed.

"I think we went in and out a couple of times and were hiding," he recalled. "All of a sudden, somebody locked us in. Just for fifteen minutes. But we were laughing for a while."

That year, Stephen entered both the Showmanship and Breed classes at the fair.

"It's all about conditioning and showmanship," explained Stephen. "The judges would know if you were working with the animal or not—the heifer, the horse, the oxen."

In Showmanship, the judges look at how you set your animal up, if you keep it clean, if you lead it well and if the animal fights the halter or reins. In the Breed class, judges look at how well the animal stands, its markings, its size, its stature and its form.

"You have to set the animal up for the judges," said Stephen. "If your animal has an udder, one leg has to be forward when the judges are on one side and then you have to move your animal again when the judge goes to the other side."

"When I won champion there, I showed twin calves, Sandy and Candy. They were Holstein animals, twin heifers," Stephen said. "It's not often you'll get twin heifers; oftentimes they will be male and female."

When twins are male and female, the female is a freemartin—infertile—so a dairy farmer would not keep that animal for the herd.

Some of the 4-H participants would sell their cows when they reached maturity because their families didn't have milking herds. When the Twisting Hillbillies became a dairy and beef club, some kids watched their animals auctioned off for slaughter.

"Wow. I can't believe they can do that," Stephen would think. "You know, you lose a puppy, it's bad. You lose a goldfish, as a kid. I say, the larger the animal the more it hurts."

Stephen feels lucky his twin Holsteins went into his family's Castle Hill Farm's milking herd.

"Even if they weren't in 4-H, a lot of farm kids raised their animals," said Alyce Block. "They became their pets, too. They'd be able to jump on a cow's back just like they could jump on a horse, if they trained them like that from little."

OX PULL CONTEST

Farmers came from all over New England to compete in the ox pull contest. In the mid-1950s, forty-four yokes of oxen competed.

"We got paid so much for being there, and then [you received prize money] if you won," said Charles Ferris III of Ferris Acres Farm in Newtown. "Didn't everybody go to Danbury. It was almost a select group because there wasn't enough room to hold everybody over there at the barns. We went every year."

Charles's father had a pair of oxen that weighed under 2,800 pounds and was never beaten in that class, he said.

The ox pull, or draw, was held at Blue Ribbon Stadium. A pair of oxen would be hitched to a stone boat made out of planks and sawed up at an angle. These were generally five or six feet long and three or more feet wide. The weights—field stones in the early fair years and concrete blocks later on—were added incrementally to the stone boat.

The contest was divided into classes by weight of the animals, and the heavier the class, the more weight was initially loaded onto the sled-like stone boats. A light class might start with 750 pounds, Charles said.

"Now my father's [team] would pull 9,600 pounds at some fairs—but not all fairs," said Charles Ferris. "A lot depends on the weather—if it's a damp day and the pits have been wet down, they'll pull more. A dry pit had friction."

The fair, said Charles, was his father's *really* big thing. He took his vacation during Danbury Fair Week, and everything he did during the rest of the year was about going to the fair.

"Before he was married he walked his cattle to fairs—from Newtown to Goshen and to Bethlehem fairs," said Charles, shaking his head. "Can you imagine that?"

This same generation of farmers sent out Christmas postcards featuring photographs of their oxen. When horses started to replace oxen on farms, many of these same farmers kept a pair of oxen for competition, for logging or, like Charles's father, to haul the milk cans to the road.

"In the olden days, the ox people would come around during the spring and summer, knock on your door and visit you. That was a social call," said Charles. "They'd talk over the old times and talk about people they knew and how they were health-wise. The men would be dressed respectfully and [would] always take their hats off when they went into a house or in front of a woman."

It took all summer to prepare an ox for the ox pull, said Charles. He'd work with them every day pulling a stone boat with weights at the family farm to toughen up the cattle's necks and build up their legs. Like all farmers, he began to train the animals when they were young and didn't let them pull too much until they matured.

The ox pull was held most days but not on Wednesday, when the oxen were in the daily parade, thus dubbed the Cattle Parade of Champions. Through midcentury, horses had the pulling stage on the last weekend of the fair. The horses, Charles remembered, would get "rowdy" so they eliminated that contest and replaced it with more ox pulling.

Wayne Allen, the superintendent of cattle and oxen, would announce on the loudspeaker who was pulling, how much weight was on the boat, what the cattle weighed and who owned them. Allen owned a 350-acre dairy farm in Vermont and judged and exhibited all over New England. Prior to becoming superintendent at the Danbury Fair, he had shown his cattle, primarily Holstein, at Blue Ribbon Stadium for two decades.

Charles D. Ferris Jr. won many blue ribbons in the ox pull competition's under-2,800-pound class. His team pulled as much as 9,600 pounds. *Charles D. Ferris III.*

"No one has ever come near the professionalism of Wayne Allen," said Charles Ferris, recalling the announcer's snappy, crisp voice. "He had a good voice on the microphone, good Vermont accent to go with it."

Similar to the stock car racing devotees, fans filled Blue Ribbon Stadium to root for their favorite farmer or team. Sometimes it was simply a matter of local pride, and the cheers went up for the contestants from a spectator's hometown.

"I used to watch the oxen—that was a big thing there," said farmer Stephen Paproski of Newtown. "The Ferrises were big-time into oxen. You had Percy Ferris, Billy Ferris, Charlie Ferris Sr. and Jr.

"Some people—not the Ferrises—didn't training them properly," he said. "I remember women getting up screaming because they were hitting them with the whips. The Humane Society came up and stopped the guy."

Farmers who respected their animals would sometimes concede the contest and be satisfied with second or third place in order to prevent injury to their animals.

Charles Ferris and his father trained their oxen so well that they responded not only to the usual voice commands of *Hah!* (left) and *Gee!* (right) but also to a touch on the front or rear.

The ox pull was a contest of strength as well as handling and strategy and was rarely a matter of oxen pulling the boat forward in a straight line.

The rewards?

"Monetarily, nothing probably," said Charles, who took top honors in the under 3,200-pound oxen draw with his pair of Holsteins, Ted and Ned. "But you had a sense of pride at the skill at maneuvering your cattle to get the boat all the way out."

Unlike his father, who judged cattle and worked the ox pull contest his entire life, Charles III stopped participating in fair events early on. That was partly because more hobbyist-farmers were competing, but he also needed to tend to his dairy herd, which needed milking each morning and evening.

"I couldn't stand being away from the farm too long," he said. "I also had to cut corn at that time of year. I felt negligent or something going to the fair."

THE DAILY PARADE

C. Irving Jarvis Sr. arranged the parade for each day. The route wound through the entire fairground, and the crowd simply parted as a jeep-drawn tram, orchestras, marching bands, Clydesdales, Royal Mounted Police, clowns, elephants, statesmen, cattle, sheep, oxen and a whole host of winged, four-legged, striped and spotted performers gaily passed by.

"I just can't believe Leahy was able to pull off a parade every day with 300,000 people there for Fair Week," said Millie Godfrey, whose uncle drove Wendell Cook's band in the event. "This huge parade going through the fairground with all these people."

Elephants were part of the daily parade. Charles Ferris recalled the elephants were housed in a barn next to the cattle.

"They'd take a couple or three out every day—big ones—and go up around to the grandstand and come back again. They had chains on their feet," he said. "I was scared—I was a small kid then."

Young Charles devised a plan in the event that the elephants got loose and stampeded.

After John W. Leahy died, Fred Fearn, pictured here in the parade, became president and general manager of the fair, and John Stetson became vice-president and secretary. *From* The Newtown Bee.

The parade traveled right through the crowded fairground and included elephants, circus performers, Queen's coach, the Hay Ride tram and even ostriches. The Clydesdales pulling the Budweiser wagon were favorites. *From* The Newtown Bee.

The fair often highlighted other cultures. Princess Goldenrod and her husband, both Penobscot Indians, performed tribal dances on the Big Top Stage and rode in every parade for years. *From* The Newtown Bee.

"I had my mind made up I'd go down to the ox pull ring, where there were bleachers backed up to this big cement," he said. "I'd go up the bleachers and onto the roof, and they wouldn't be able to get me that way."

Wednesday, Governor's Day, was the Parade of Champions when all livestock strutted through the fairground. Charles would walk his oxen from the barns to the front of the grandstand, where Wayne Allen, superintendent of cattle and oxen, introduced Leahy and then each individual in the parade.

11

Home Arts Show

Sewing, Baking and Canning

The Danbury Fair's premium categories for pies, jams, pickles, etc. were eliminated in later years. Some say that's because there was too much fussing in the old days when the women did not approve of the judges' decisions.
—New York Times, *September 30, 1977*

Whether your talents coalesced in the mixing bowl or on the quilt rack, the fair's Home Arts Show was the place to show off your handiwork and, perhaps, win a little pocket money. When New England Village was built, the national and local competitions were housed in its Town Hall.

In 1961, the Premium List—the list of awards, that is—for baking included divisions for various yeast breads, "dietetic" baking, birthday cakes, wedding cakes and lemon meringue pies, all made from scratch. The clothing division included embroidery, hemstitching, stuffed toys, doilies, potholders and blouses, and the canning divisions were all manner of vegetables and fruits and jellies.

The rules were straightforward: Work must be completed within the twelve months immediately prior to the fair. All work must be "owned and done" by the entrant. All awards were on the basis of merit. Premiums could be withheld if there was a lack of competition and/or the judges deemed the exhibits "unworthy."

Smaller items required more than one example per entry. Bakers were to provide six Parkerhouse rolls or raised doughnuts, twelve pieces of candy or six bar cookies; canners, three jars of string beans. Jam/jelly entries that were in "sticky or dirty jars" would be eliminated from competition, according to the 1961 premium list.

The fair hosted a children's canning class and a "Men Only" crochet class. Only Connecticut residents were allowed to enter the national contests; residents of the tri-state area could enter the local contests.

Olga Paproski of Newtown entered many categories of domestic arts, including jams and jellies, which called for three jars in each entry. Olga grew raspberries and currants for canning on the dairy and Christmas tree farm where she and her husband, Sam, lived.

"We'd go over to Palestine Road and pick blackberries for the jam, and I'd get all scratched up," recalled her son, Stephen. "I'm sure she did win for her jams, but she was a seamstress. Sewing was a big thing for her."

Olga won ribbons and a little prize money for her blouses, dresses and skirts, he said. In 1963, she won the "Best of Fair" award and a Singer sewing machine for her skilled work and had her picture in the paper.

Singer offered a sewing machine and set of attachments, a year of free service and a sewing course to the person who won the Blue Ribbon Rosette Award in the Home Arts sewing competition. Other companies, such as flour manufacturers, also provided special incentives.

Stephen said one of the main reasons his mother entered the contests was she would get free admission tickets and her family could enjoy the fair when financial constraints would not allow that otherwise.

"But she liked competing," said Stephen.

He recalled that when he was eight years old, his mother asked him to take her three best apple pies from their house to the car on the day entries were due at the fair.

"I went to put them in the car trunk and the car was locked. So I set the pies half on the trunk and half on the fender and went to get the keys," he said. "When I opened the trunk, they *all* flipped over.

"My mom was strict years ago," he laughed, "and I was so afraid to go in the house."

Shirley Ferris, former Connecticut commissioner of agriculture, also entered both sewing and baking contests. She started entering the contests when she was nineteen or twenty years old. And she always had her eye on the blue ribbon.

The first year she entered an apple pie, she won fourth place. The next year, with the same pie recipe, she won third and the following year, second place.

"So, I thought, 'Well, fourth year's the charm,'" Shirley said. "I entered it again only some little old lady entered an absolutely perfect strawberry pie. And the year after that, they didn't have the contests any more. They [took] the building with all the tomatoes, relishes and the jams and all that and filled it with vendors."

Shirley would study the Premium list sent out long before Fair Week and decide what she would enter that particular year. One year, she entered a dress she had made for her daughter, then four years old. She thought it was quite nice and was surprised she didn't win any prize for it, so she asked the judge about it.

"I had used iron-on tape at the hem, not realizing that I shouldn't have been doing that," she said. "So I was disqualified."

Shirley did get her share of blue ribbons at the Danbury Fair, however, including one for Grandma's Prize-Winning Gingerbread. The fair wasn't as much fun, she said, after they eliminated the Home Arts competition.

Grandma's Prize-Winning Gingerbread

2½ cups all-purpose flour, sifted
1 teaspoon baking powder
1 teaspoon salt
1 teaspoon ground ginger
2 teaspoons ground cinnamon
½ teaspoon ground cloves
½ cup vegetable shortening
½ cup sugar
¾ teaspoon baking soda
1 cup molasses
2 eggs
1 cup hot water

Sift flour, baking powder, salt and spices together. Cream shortening, sugar and baking soda. Add molasses. Stir in ½ cup dry ingredients. Add eggs; beat well. Add hot water and remaining dry ingredients, ⅓ cup at a time; beat by hand about 30 seconds. Pour into greased and floured 9-inch square baking pan. Bake at 350 degrees for 45 minutes. Delicious with whipped cream or slightly soft vanilla ice cream. Easy to make and keep ahead (if you hide it); makes the whole house smell good. Yield: 9 (3-inch square) servings.

12

Special at the Fair

Queens, Veterans, Students and Governors

Leahy turned down the request for free tickets, but this year, the fair chief made no bones about the reason for his refusal—that Fair visitors came to have a good time 'and didn't want to see a bunch of cripples' to remind them of the horrors of war!
—*the* Herald, *October 1948*

The Queen of the Fair was a modern-day tradition that added a little glamour to the fair. Each year, a local girl acted as a good-will ambassador with dignitaries, exhibitors and vendors. She rode in the Queen's Coach and sat on a throne where she was attended by one or two young men in uniform.

Prior to the mid-'60s, the Queen was chosen by John Leahy or C. Irving Jarvis. After that time, the winner of the Miss Danbury competition appeared as Queen.

"It was the honor to do it," said Marlene Berry Patren, who was Queen in 1961 and 1962. "There was no contest. It just happened that John Leahy knew my grandmother, and he knew me because I sat behind him in St. Joseph's Church."

One Sunday, he turned to her and asked if she wanted to be Queen of the Fair. Marlene was a junior in high school at the time, and her royal designation enabled her to get out of school early during the ten days of the fair.

"It was really fun," she recalled. "I had to wear a gown and tiara. The second year, I wore a white gown with a blue velvet jacket."

Marlene was in the parade, held at two o'clock, each day of Fair Week. The parade ended at the grandstand, where she was announced and gave a

Marlene Berry Patren was Queen of the Danbury Fair in 1961 and 1962. Although she was a "city girl," she had an affinity for cows and oxen. *Photograph by Frank R. Fonaseca. Marlene (Berry) Patren.*

speech. If there were any dignitaries in attendance, such as Governor Dempsey on Governor's Day, Marlene would greet them and sit with them in the grandstand box.

"Sixteen years old and doing this," she said. "It was pretty exciting!"

Marlene toured the Big Top, speaking to the people at the booths there. She also schmoozed with the cows and oxen and was happy to pose with a blue-ribbon bovine.

"I love cows, so I wasn't afraid or anything," she said. "I was used to them."

When Marlene was in sixth grade, she spent a week at a friend's farm in New Milford, where she took care of a cow and showed it in 4-H at the Bridgewater Fair. But she was taken to the side right away by the judges.

Beginning in the mid-1960s, the role of Queen was filled by the reigning Miss Danbury. Fairgoers would greet the Queen here at her throne or test out her seat and dream of wearing the tiara themselves. *From* The Newtown Bee.

"I was so upset," she said. "I thought, 'Oh my god, I didn't even get to show my cow!'"

It turns out Marlene was pulled aside because she was hands-down the winner—and of *two* blue ribbons.

"Everyone else was a farm kid, and they were like, 'You're a city girl and you shouldn't be doing this!'" she laughed. "And since then, I've just loved cows. I can't help it. They are so adorable—their faces and everything."

Being Queen definitely had its perks, she said. Besides free entrance tickets and money toward a gown, Queens could avoid all the usual parking hassles and park in a reserved spot near the gate.

SPECIAL DAYS

Danbury Day, which later was know as a day for students, began as a citywide holiday on Saturday, October 6, 1906. Shops closed so all residents could enjoy going to the fair, and 16,800 turned out that day despite poor weather.

Saturday later became Old Timer's Day, but sometime after 1956, it was Family Day. And the Friday of Fair Week, when the Danbury students had a holiday from school for the express purpose of attending the fair, became known as Danbury Day.

Designation of other days of the week changed according to the promotional strategy of John Leahy. Sunday was Pioneer Day and then Empire State Day to "afford an opportunity for friends from Westchester, Putnam and Dutchess Counties, as well as New York City and its several boroughs to meet," according to a press release from the fair office. Monday of the fair was Tri-County Day, "set apart for residents of Fairfield, Litchfield and New Haven Counties to co-mingle."

Veterans Day

Veterans had been given free admission to the fair for twenty-six years when John Leahy ceased this practice in 1946. Two reasons appear to be behind this

Queen of the Fair was an honor bestowed on a local high school or college woman. Her role was good-will ambassador to dignitaries, concessionaires and fairgoers alike. She had a throne, carriage and escort. *Danbury Museum & Historical Society Authority.*

decision: an effort to create the illusion of a carefree environment after the war and to stop the historical hemorrhaging of funds by giving away passes.

As Danbury welcomed back its war heroes, residents rebuked Leahy for denying them free passes. He was reported to have told the public to "stop the sentimental nonsense."

Two more years went by. The Veterans of Foreign Wars tried to intervene, but John Leahy wouldn't be swayed. Fair management fanned the fire by continuing to make comments in the newspapers, such as: "What pleasure could the blind get from attending the Fair?" and wounded veterans would "spoil the fun" of people attending the fair.

The controversy escalated into the national press, giving John W. Leahy and his Danbury Fair more attention than it had ever received. The press was not kind.

Headlines read, "Crippled? Don't Attend the Fair!" and "Blind Can't Enjoy Fair? Sully Replies."

Finally, the VFW worked with a local chapter to raise private funds to pay the entrance fee to the fair. The *Herald* printed scathing remarks in October 1948:

> So once again...the "Great" Danbury Fair played host to a group of disabled veterans who had proved their devotion to America in two bloody wars. They seemed to have themselves a dandy time in spite of the fact that they jarred against the artistic perception of the top dog on the grounds.
>
> Or perhaps I do Leahy an injustice. Once their admission fee had gravitated into his coffers, he may have been perfectly willing to have them on the grounds.

In what the *Herald* called "an ironic touch," the sideshows operator Buck Shows offered all visiting veterans free admission to its attractions that year.

Leahy defended himself against the bad press by saying he had invested a great deal of his own money to improve the fairground, build new attractions and bring in fine entertainment.

Admission into the fair was the main source of revenue for the Danbury Fair Inc. While concessionaires paid for space on the fairground and Leahy charged on weekends for the grandstand show, it was primarily the gate receipts that kept the fair afloat.

John Leahy had bought up all the shares of fair stock so he would have complete control over the operation and so he could begin to curtail the number of free admissions into the fair each year. Stockholders each had a free annual pass to the event.

His "aversion to free passes" was chronicled in the *New York World-Telegram* on September 10, 1951.

It was a policy "strange to the entertainment business and which nettles a number of people around Danbury," the article said. "[John Leahy] thinks if his fair is worth coming to, it's worth paying for, and would gladly pay his own way into one of the exhibits of which he's proudest."

Sometime during the next few years, Leahy and the veterans' groups made up, although the fair never hosted another Veterans Day. In 1950, Leahy appeared in the *News-Times* as a recipient of a citation for his "continued and untiring interest in the welfare" of disabled veterans in the region. In 1969, veterans' admission to the fair was sponsored by two organizations "in cooperation" with John Leahy.

Danbury Day for Students

A similar uproar occurred that first year the fair opened after the war when Danbury students were told they would *not* get their Friday off from school, nor would they get free passes into the fair or half-priced tickets for rides. Culpability for this decision is a bit nebulous, but it seems to be something that was agreed on by the school superintendent and the fair manager with the free-pass aversion.

That didn't sit well with the teens of the city.

"We all looked forward to that Friday of Fair Week," said Millie Godfrey. "Danbury Fair was a big thing growing up."

When word got out about Friday reverting to a regular school day, the youth met with school officials and asked to have Danbury Day reinstated. When that didn't work, the students attempted to negotiate half a day off from school that Friday. The board of education stood firm, and the students simmered.

"We were hurt by it," said Connie McGowan, who was a student at Danbury High School at the time. "They'd have the governor there and all. What about the kids? Why can't we enjoy it? Why can't we have the day off?"

The students didn't have an institution like the VFW behind them, but they had equal conviction, the energy of youth and (they believed) justice on their side.

"It was something we felt strongly we were entitled to," said Connie. "So a whole bunch of us decided we were going to strike the school and walk up to the fair and *demand* that Leahy give us a free pass to go to the fair."

THE GREAT DANBURY STATE FAIR

The press called it "smouldering juvenile resentment" that "flamed into open rebellion" that Friday, October 4, 1946. At least 1,200 students boycotted school. Only 100 were found at their desks that morning when the superintendent raced over to the school after seeing crowds of students protesting on Main Street.

Of those involved in the strike, two to three hundred youth stayed outside on the school grounds. The same amount simply skipped school to attend the fair on their own dime, and at least eight hundred marched through town singing school songs and carrying placards that stated "It's Our Fair" and "School or Serfdom."

The students marched from White Street, where the high school was located in the 1940s, to the center of town only to find the superintendent out of his office. The group split up to look for the official and, not finding him, continued en masse to the fairground.

"As we went down White Street, the cars were blowing their horns, and people were clapping," said Millie Godfrey, who participated in the march.

The students walked three miles to the fair gates, where they surged forward and shouted to be let in. The sheer number of them at the gate hindered other fairgoers from getting through.

On October 4, 1946, students marched from the high school on White Street through downtown Danbury (pictured during the 1940s in this postcard image) and to the fairground to demand that their holiday and free passes to the fair be reinstated. *Newtown Historical Society.*

"We demanded we get into the fair; we didn't care if we got expelled," said Connie McGowan. "We did it in a very nice manner, but we were fighting for what we believed in."

Leahy would not open the gates for the students until the superintendent approved the day off from school. Finally, word came through that all grades were given a holiday. Parochial schools followed suit. That afternoon two thousand city youths passed through the gates of the fair for free.

"Eventually, Mr. Leahy—one of the finest gentlemen in Danbury—opened the gates," said Connie. "He felt he owed the City of Danbury this. We won."

Danbury Day on the Friday of Fair Week continued until the fair closed in 1981. Both elementary and high schools students in the city had the day off and were admitted to the fairground for free. By 1956, the number of passes given to city youth was seven thousand.

"I still recall waiting for that wonderful moment when the passes were finally handed out," said Elaine Lagarto, who grew up in the city. "Danbury School Day Friday was always the day we waited for all year. In the weeks just prior to that special school holiday, the excitement could be felt building."

"Kids who went to St. Peter's in Danbury but lived in Bethel would still get free tickets," said lifelong Danbury resident Paul Trudel. "They'd go back home and say to their friends, 'I got free tickets to the fair!' Some people it bothered."

Hilda Nichols, who lived in Bethel, said she didn't care. Hilda *loved* the fair and wasn't about to miss the fun.

"I'd skip school that Friday because I didn't have the day off like they did in Danbury," she said. "I'd pay to get in."

Judy Menegay Schoonmaker also skipped school in Bethel to go to the fair, but she got in for free because she had a cousin in Danbury with extra tickets.

"Some of her school friends wouldn't go, so my sister and I—and other cousins, too—would go to her house in Danbury, and we either walked or took the bus to the fair," she said. "We'd spend the whole day at the fairgrounds, and my mother would pick us up after work."

"When we were going to school we didn't have money in our pockets. I don't remember going on rides," recalled Millie Godfrey. "But you could walk around all day long and not spend a cent and have a terrific time. I'm talking about the early 1940s when I was a teenager. There was so much to see. You'd see all the kids from school. And we thought we were so terrific because we managed to pull this off. Big shots!"

To many children and families, the Danbury Fair was the event of the year.

"You'd get a new outfit to go to the fair," recalled Marlene Patren, who was a youth in Danbury in the 1950s and '60s. "I remember in seventh grade getting a new pair of wool Bermuda shorts and penny loafers and high knee socks. You'd meet your friends and go for the day."

Governor's Day

Wednesday became Governor's Day, which appears to be a tradition started by John Leahy right after the war. Honorees were welcomed by John Leahy and were given gifts from farmers who exhibited at the fair, ribbons and lots of photo opportunities.

The governor and his entourage would then hop on the tram known as the "Hay Ride"—a string of cars drawn by a jeep—and join the parade to the grandstand. Here he gave a speech and then sat with Queen of the fair in one of the boxes to enjoy the grandstand show.

Prior to 1974, when Ella Grasso was elected governor, the press took an inordinate interest in what the governors' wives wore to the fair down to the

The parade ended at the grandstand, and before the show, Governor O'Neill offered a few words to the audience. *Danbury Museum & Historical Society Authority.*

This crowd has gathered not just to meet Governor McConaughy but also to see the bear standing in front of him. The governor's wife and daughter are on either side of him. *State Archives, Connecticut State Library.*

jewelry around their necks. Likewise, every move of the governor on the Wednesday of Fair Week was documented in detail.

Governor James McConaughy attended the fair in 1947 with his wife, Elizabeth, and daughter, Phoebe. Among his other stops at the fair, he and his wife enjoyed a square dance set in the Big Top, watched the circus grandstand show, viewed a prize Guernsey cow and bought a book of raffle tickets at the American Legion booth. McConaughy died the next spring of influenza and did not finish his first term as governor.

During his tour of the fair in 1955, Governor Abraham Ribicoff put in a plea for the redevelopment of the russet apple, which was no longer being grown for the market. The *News-Times* reported on October 6, "Farmers have found that the public will only buy red apples."

Ribicoff marveled at a remote control–powered mower demonstrated by a vendor lounging in a nearby chair. The governor's last official act of the day was to feed straw to Corrisdale sheep in the Sheep Barn.

This trained bear stands up to greet Governor McConnaughy and his daughter, Phoebe, during the 1947 Danbury Fair. *State Archives, Connecticut State Library.*

"All my brothers and sisters and cousins would vie for the opportunity to be the one to present the governor with a gift basket," said Cathy Bronson, a seventh-generation Hurlbut family farmer in Roxbury. "The basket represented what we had on the farm, any vegetable you can think of that would grow in this area we grow—lettuces, cabbages and beets, carrots, and onions, peppers, tomatoes, eggplant."

John Dempsey followed Ribicoff as governor of Connecticut. This gregarious Irishman thoroughly enjoyed his visits to the fair and, on one occasion, picked up the baton and led the band with great vigor.

In 1976, at lunch with Rotarians prior to visiting the fair, Governor Ella Grasso remarked, "One of the joys of autumn in Connecticut is the opportunity to take part in the Governor's Day ceremonies at the Danbury Fair."

Another special guest of John Leahy's, Senator Joseph McCarthy, arrived by plane at the neighboring airport. Always the showman, the fair owner asked if Senator McCarthy would like to ride an elephant. Having just had surgery, McCarthy declined. He did have a sip of beer when a spectator offered him his glass and submitted to a weight guess by Dan Burke, who had been exercising this gift at the Danbury Fair for forty years.

Opposite, top: Fair owner John Leahy wanted everyone, including governors, to have fun at his fair. Here, Governor Dempsey conducts the band at the grandstand show. *Danbury Museum & Historical Society Authority.*

Opposite, bottom: Ella Grasso, the first woman elected as governor in her own right, greets the crowd as a jeep-drawn tram called the Hayride ushers her along the parade route. *Photograph by Robert Mannion. Danbury Museum & Historical Authority.*

13

Fair Figures

Giants, Reindeer and Pixies, Oh, My!

In 1992, I got a phone call at 6:30 one morning that Uncle Sam was laying
[sic] down in the parking lot. And I said, "Is this a crank call?" And he said,
"No, this is Robbie, your caretaker!"
—Jack Gillette, owner of the Magic Forest, Lake George, New York

The 1961 fair program included a little box with these words: "Bring Your Camera: 1001 Photogenic Statues and Interesting Subjects to Photograph." The giant statues are icons of the Danbury Fair, and the best known is Farmer John.

The theme for the 1957 fair was "Farmer John Comes to the Fair," and two new figures dressed in jeans and straw hats greeted visitors. They had slightly different poses, and one became known as the *real* Farmer John and the other as his brother.

Every child knew if he got lost somewhere on the 142-acre fairground, he was to wait at the foot of Farmer John until his parents claimed him. This was also the spot where locals would meet up with friends from New York.

Sometimes, the nearly thirty-foot-tall farmer wore fabric clothes, but most years, he'd be found near the Big Top in overalls painted right on his body. He was in good company with a handful of other giants and a thousand smaller figures dancing, riding and perching on roofs throughout the fairground: dinosaurs, ice-cream men, hippopotamus, can-can dancers, Dutch figures, cowboys, dwarves, pixies, Cinderella, elephants, glass blowers, roosters, skunks, fairies, pigs, eagles, bears, geese, fairy-tale characters, archers, clowns, snowmen, reindeer—the list goes on.

Farmer John and his twin brother, each thirty feet tall, were made for the 1957 fair. Children knew if they got lost they should wait for their parents by John's big feet. *From* The Newtown Bee.

Where did these come from? And where did they go?

Some of the figures John Leahy bought secondhand. Sixty of his pixies had first decorated the city of Chicago. Santa with his reindeer first rang in the holidays in a Midwest department store. Peppermint sticks three stories tall had been part of an outdoors Christmas display arranged by Macy's, Gimbels and Saks Fifth Avenue in New York City; Leahy bought these and had painted on them "The Sweetest Fair in New England."

Many figures were purchased from Messmore and Daman, a New York company that specialized in fabricating chicken wire and papier mâché sculpture. In the 1920s, they offered grandly executed parade floats with

Above: The giant figures became iconic of the Great Danbury State Fair and could be seen on the horizon as you approached the fair from any direction. *From* The Newtown Bee.

Left: Fair maintenance foreman Gordon Nichols sets up an elephant figure, likely for the P.T. Barnum Museum. *Danbury Museum and Historical Society Authority.*

historical themes. During the next decade, the company became innovators in mechanizing figures, such as the forty-eight-foot dinosaur exhibited at the 1933–34 Century of Progress World's Fair in Chicago. The four-thousand-pound creature could flick its tail, twist it's neck, roll its eyes and pick up a woman by clamping its foam rubber teeth around her. Two men on a wooden platform inside the dinosaur operated electric motors controlling these functions, according to the October 1931 issue of *Popular Science*.

Messmore and Daman sold its innovative sculptures to department stores for window displays and to amusement parks. It is likely John Leahy had the company fashion the mechanical elephant for his P.T. Barnum exhibit.

International Fiberglass of Venice, California, provided John Leahy with unpainted molded fiberglass pieces with which he had his staff create figures, such as Paul Bunyan. The company also made dinosaur replicas for the 1964 Danbury Fair.

As Leahy expanded his ideas for the fair, so did he enlarge his staff to include resident craftsmen to design and fabricate figures and villages. Peter Reilly, a New York–based artist who had studied at the Pennsylvania Academy of Fine Arts in Philadelphia, lived in a "vine-covered cottage" on the Danbury fairground for six months during each year between 1967 and 1979. In a loft workshop in New England Village, he created hundreds of pieces for the fair, including the figures and backdrop for Cinderellaland, Robinson Crusoe and family and Rip Van Winkle. He also painted murals for indoor displays.

Peter Reilly often worked with two other artisans on the Danbury Fair payroll, artist Francis "Pete" Farnum and carpenter Richard Waterbury. The three worked together to create figures, such as the forty-foot-tall Buffalo Bill, but also attractions like the Pirates' Den.

By 1974, just about halfway through his residency, Reilly had fashioned 150 figures out of fiberglass, chicken wire and celastic, a German product similar to but more weather resistant than papier mâché. In a *News-Times* article from Sunday, April 17, 1983, Reilly recalled being asked by John Leahy if his salary was "sufficient." The artist responded: "I should be paying you for all the fun I'm having!"

During the off-seasons, Leahy used figures from the Danbury Fair to enhance his billboard display on White Street, Danbury. Giant bunnies stood as sentinels at Easter; Santa and the white reindeer had the attention of every child who passed at Christmastime.

When the fair closed and all the figures were up for sale, Jack Gillette purchased about six hundred of them for his Magic Forest Amusement Park in Lake

Resident artists wrapped celastic around chicken wire to create unique and memorable pieces for the fair. *From* The Newtown Bee.

The Canadian Woodsman guarded the hot dog and root beer stand. Every year, the figures were touched up before the gates to the fair opened. *Photograph by Judy (Menegay) Schoonmaker.*

George, New York. This cache includes the Three Little Pigs, Goldilocks and the Three Bears, Robinson Crusoe, bears standing on three legs, twenty pirates, forty-eight pixies, Dr. Doolittle and the llama, snowmen, Rip Van Winkle, Humpty Dumpty, Noah's Ark, Hansel and Gretel, tigers, cougars, elephants, giraffes, Smokey the Bear and Buckingham Palace guards.

Many pieces Jack bought were made by Peter Reilly. After transporting them to New York, the amusement park owner asked the artist, then in his

Large fiberglass figures, know as "Muffler Men," were popular advertisement for roadway businesses. A staff of artists and carpenters made them into folk heroes of the fair. *Danbury Museum and Historical Society Authority.*

late sixties, to come to Lake George to refresh his creations and help Jack set them up.

Jack remembers Reilly's reaction when he saw the structure Jack had built to house his complete Cinderellaland.

"He said these figures were his 'children,' and he was so happy to get his 'family' back together in one space," recalled Jack Gillette. "Nice man."

Reilly wanted his figures to have a natural expression, to interact with one another, if he was creating a scene. He might study photographs of his subject, or he might create something from his imagination. He loved working at the Danbury Fair because John Leahy and assistant general manager Fred Fearn gave him artistic license.

Reilly often used chicken wire and other materials to create the structure for his figures. The celastic dries hard and is fairly weather resistant. "But the trouble is, when it gets wet, it rots out the stuff behind it that you used for the form of the figure," said Jack Gillette. "The stuff that is outside just deteriorates as time goes on."

But anything made of celastic he has indoors, such as the animal band, is as good as the day he bought it, he said. Jack also bought all the extra celastic material offered at the auction to make repairs, which, he said, was "one of my brighter moves."

Jack has many other pieces by Reilly, including the Old Woman in the Shoe, nine reindeer, Little Boy Blue, Ichabod Crane and the Headless Horseman. The iconic thirty-six-foot Uncle Sam is in his parking lot, but Gillette had some delicate political maneuvering to do to get that particular figure situated at the Magic Forest.

"Lake George was giving me a hard time because I wanted to put it in the parking lot and they considered it a sign. I went back and forth with them for months," said Jack.

The zoning department wanted Uncle Sam behind the main fence of the amusement park and reminded Jack Gillette about the Adirondack Park height limitation of forty feet. Friends of Jack's decided they would protest at town hall if zoning "would not let Uncle Sam stand on his own two feet."

But that wasn't the end of Uncle Sam's trouble.

One night, after being installed in the amusement park lot, Uncle Sam was pulled over by some mischievous youth; he was discovered broken off at the ankles, lying in the parking lot.

"I got a friend to come over with a pay loader," said Jack. "We strapped it up in pieces and took it over to the workshop a quarter mile behind the park."

Above: The structural lines on the Old Woman's Shoe indicate that it was made by fair artisans, as opposed to the smooth surface of the fiberglass cow. *Photograph by Judy (Menegay) Schoonmaker.*

Left: The Magic Forest Amusement Park in Lake George, New York, has more than six hundred figures from the fair, including Uncle Sam. *From* The Newtown Bee.

More than one thousand figures delighted fairgoers. A very few of them remained local, like this trapeze artist that continues to soar in Rosie Tomorrow's restaurant in Danbury. *From* The Newtown Bee.

It took eight days with four people working on the figure to repair and secure it with a steel post so Uncle Sam couldn't be toppled again. "It was a lot of work repainting the whole thing. I had to run about twenty-five miles away to get resin and cloth because there was nothing left around the area," said Jack. "We sand everything right down to the bare fiberglass, then we repaint it. We use automotive paint."

Hundreds of other figures were scattered all over the region. Private collectors and restauranteurs—many now gone—purchased figures at the auction.

The owner of Rosy Tomorrow's in Danbury bought figures and decorated the restaurant with them: a trapeze artist and airplane suspended from the ceiling, a lion that roars on a raised platform, a fortuneteller and other figures tucked in corners throughout the building. Outside mounted on the building is the sign "This Is the Happiest Fairground in the World; Come Again Next Year." Strangely, it bears the date 1981, the year the fair closed.

The thirty-foot-tall Viking and twenty-five-foot cowboy figures were purchased by Benson's Animal Park in New Hampshire. The Danbury Fair's Queen's coach, Frosty the Snowman, Robin Hood and all the international figures John Leahy had purchased at the 1964 World's Fair went there, too. Benson's closed in 1987 and had its own auction.

"One of the Indian figures is in Maine, right off 295 between Exit 17 and 20, you can see it," said Judy Schoonmaker.

Another Indian is now overlooking the Riverhead Raceway on Long Island. But that accounts for just two of at least five Indians, including the twenty-foot-tall Chief Mohawk who stood at the entrance of Goldtown.

Beardsley Zoo in Bridgeport, Connecticut, bought a giant rabbit for its duck pen. A miniature golf concession at the beach in South Norwalk purchased an over-sized fiberglass cow. The St. Louis Museum of Transportation is reported to have paid $42,000 at the auction for the 1858 Daniel Nason steam engine.

The carousel was dismantled and the pieces sold individually to bring the highest price.

Farmer John was purchased by United House Wrecking in Stamford and kept on display outside for many years. The owners repaired the figure numerous times before it deteriorated so much it couldn't be salvaged.

"We talk about the Danbury Fair sometimes when we get together," said Jill Austin about family gatherings. "We scratch our head and say, 'Does anyone know what happened to Paul Bunyan?'"

14

The Outer Limits

Gypsies, Freaks and Hootchy-Kootchy Girls

For one minute—that's all folks, just one single minute—I'm going to let you—you and you and you—into this greatest of shows, this monument of strange people and objects—for just one minute. I'm going to let you in for only 25 cents—only a quarter of a dollar—just 25 cents. Don't dally now, folks. Step right up!
—Justin Wagner, sideshow barker, Danbury News-Times, *October 1, 1957*

In the early years, the Midway was home to the fortunetellers and sideshows with fire-eaters and "freaks of nature." In 1899, pious members of the Danbury community wanted to scour the fair clean, and they petitioned the Law and Order League to shut down these acts.

Not everyone agreed this was such a good idea.

"To close up the sided shows was to hurt the exhibitions," said an October 8, 1899 article in the *New York Times*. "For the great majority that attend the fair each year simply go to see the fakirs."

THE STRANGEST PEOPLE

Who could resist the Floating Lady, the 4-Armed Female Enigma, the Handcuff King, the Decapitator? The more gruesome or freakish, the bigger the draw.

Journalist John Chapman witnessed something so disturbing at the Danbury Fair that he wrote paragraphs about it in his October 6, 1946 article for the *Sunday News*: an inordinate amount of people had shelled out money and lined up to "goggle" at a polio victim in an iron lung.

"Perhaps she was just another healthy hireling, like the headless girl being kept alive by chromium tubing or the indestructible wench who gets sawed in half," he wrote. "But on the other hand, she could have been a paralysis case who hit upon a country fair as the place to make some money and defray the great cost of being kept alive."

These weird and tantalizing attractions were so popular that John Leahy allowed them to remain at the Danbury Fair for many years. They didn't exactly fit the concept of the "family fair" he was trying to promote, so he banished the strange stuff to the outskirts of the fairground.

Everyone knew they were there, and many attempted to sneak under the tents guarded by barkers.

"The last aisle at the fair—it was almost forbidden territory," said Eunice Laverty, who, like many other young adults who attended the fair, was drawn to see what was back there.

The Freak Show was on the right, she recalled, and the "Girlie Show" on left.

Attractions such as the Straight Jacket Escape, the 4-Armed Female Enigma and the Pillory Mystery filled the Midway before being relegated to the outskirts of the fairground. *Danbury Museum and Historical Society Authority.*

"Especially Catholic kids, we thought, 'Oh, this is so immodest. This is a terrible thing. We shouldn't be watching; we should be praying for them,'" she laughed. "But I think you were more afraid of someone *seeing* you go in, than going in."

She remembered each show had an elevated stage for the draws like Marlo the Mule-Faced Boy, who had "a memorable set of choppers," and the women who wore bathing suits and shuffled back and forth to Pink Onions. The idea was to entice you to *pay* to go inside the tents and see the really good stuff, the freakiest-of-the-freaks and women in some appealing stage of disrobement.

That whole skirted area of the fairground was dusty and dirty, recalled Eunice.

"When you were watching the dancing girls up there, you were looking right at their ankles," she said. "They all had dirty ankles because they had to walk back to their trailer through the dirt and nobody would wash them."

Other come-ons billed as the Strangest People included a heavily bearded lady, a sword swallower and an escape artist put in shackles and a straight jacket. Eunice said she could have stayed all day just watching these unusual people come and go off the stage.

"They were the draw outside, but the Siamese twins were inside," she said. And when she and her friends got a little older, they finally got up the nerve to pay to go inside and meet the twins.

"The tent was pretty creepy, with a dirt floor," she said. "The Siamese twins were in something like a big B&G sauerkraut jar, one of those big jars. Twins. *Ahhhhh!* We thought they were real people. We wouldn't have spent money had we known that they were in a *jar*."

Carl J. Tomanio recalled the bearded lady, the Tallest Man in the World and the Strongest Man in the World.

"It would be tough to get inside because of the hawkers outside," said Carl. "They had the Half-Man/Half-Woman who was equipped with both, who'd start to disrobe and give you a quick look."

Millie Godfrey is still annoyed that the Half-Man/Half-Woman would not perform when she and her husband, John Godfrey, paid their money for the tent show. John was wearing his Danbury Fair Police uniform, but Millie said that's not the reason the show came to a screeching halt.

"The woman wouldn't perform in front of a female, and I was the only female there," she said.

"Hey!" Millie laughed, "she could have put anything there. How would we know without examining it?"

Millie also remembered the midget and the Fat Lady. She said Fred Fearn, who became general manager of the fair after John Leahy died, didn't like the girlie shows and the freak shows.

"That was not making it a family place to be. Hootchy-kootchy girls come out and wiggle their rears and boobs, and the barker would try to get people to go inside. And those odd-ball shows," Millie said. "Fred Fearn kicked them all out; he cleaned up the fairground. It was a weird bunch."

The fair also attracted con men and pickpockets, the "low-life of the low-life." Paul Trudel remembered the gamers who cheated people.

"There were scam artists hidden in the back, doing the shell game. Not so many people knew what was going on," he said. "When Mr. Leahy found out from somebody who had lost a lot of money, he'd send the fair police down there to take the guys out."

"Unscrupulous characters would follow the fair," said Carl J. Tomanio. "You had to be aware, be careful because it was really crowded."

THE GYPSIES

"I remember as a little kid being scared to death of the gypsies," said Millie, who grew up in Danbury and is now eighty-five. "We were told not to talk to any of them."

"When we were young, we were warned to not even go out in the front of the house because the gypsies would take you," said Ann Diker, who grew up in Danbury during the late 1940s and early 1950s and was scared enough to stay in the backyard during Fair Week.

The gypsies, she was told, followed the fairs from town to town. And stole children.

Ann never saw anyone she identified as a gypsy, but she was fearful of running into one—especially at the fair.

"When I was growing up in Bethel, the gypsies used to come around in the summertime," said a ninety-year-old woman who now lives in Danbury. "They wore bandanas, colorful clothes, the women big skirts. They were very popular—they would tell your fortune at the fair. I don't know where they came from, but they were there every year until I graduated high school."

She said she and her siblings were so afraid of the gypsies that when there was a knock on the door, they would hide under the bed.

"We knew it was them!" she said. "They weren't looking for work; they were collecting money. You didn't have much money back then. You had to lock your doors because they would steal everything."

Her parents warned her the gypsies might have a "blade or something." She does not ever remember hearing that gypsies stole children.

"I know they did have a problem at the fair with them," she said. "I don't know when they disbanded them, but all of a sudden they weren't there."

THE GIRLIE SHOWS

When Garry Burdick was growing up, *Playboy* was not available to him or his best friend Stuart, and both young men were eager to see just how a woman looked. So they decided to sneak into the hootchy-kootchy tent at the Danbury Fair.

"We were around back and lifted the canvas and got in like that," Garry said. "So there we are, and the cutest little girl comes out. I say that because they weren't all ugly. And she began to take her clothes off and the St. Louie Blues were playing.

The seedier side of the fair had great staying power because the sideshows of the "Strangest People" and Girlie Show were so popular. *Photograph by Garry Camp Burdick.*

"This is the first woman," he said, putting his hand to his heart. "She was *so* beautiful. I mean I just couldn't believe there was somebody like that. And she didn't have anything on."

Although it crossed his mind, Garry never had the nerve to go back. He thought they were still trying to catch him for sneaking in.

"It was a *wonderful* experience for a boy who was thirteen or fourteen," he said. "Takes my breath away, still. Because I love women just *so* much."

15

Security

Danbury Fair Police and Pinkertons

The people would be going, "C'mon Fred! Open the Gates!! C'mon Fred!" He would blow his whistle. People would have their tickets half-ripped and hold up one hand and you'd pulled the ticket. And they'd run with their blankets to get their seats. They had to get their seats.
—*Judy Menegay Schoonmaker, Pinkerton Security at the Racearena*

When John Leahy became manager of the fair in 1946, he maintained the tradition of closing at dusk. His advertisements always included an emphatic, "No Nights" next to the hours.

Some say the fairground wasn't properly lit to have the fair operate into the evening; others believe Leahy didn't want all the problems a late-night fair would engender.

Fair attendance swelled from 127,765 to an average of 350,000 during the thirty-five years that Danbury Fair Inc. operated the event. Increased numbers of fairgoers, however, meant more lost children, more pickpockets to take advantage of the crowded venue and a lot more money sitting in the fair's treasury office.

John Leahy employed his own Danbury Fair Police force and contracted with the Pinkerton Detective Agency to provide ticket sellers, gatekeepers and people to help with crowd control. He built a headquarters on the fairground for each of these security forces. He also had the support of the Danbury Police, who operated a substation nearby.

During the 1950s, Dorothy Joselovitz belonged to the Civil Defense Auxiliary Police, which supplemented the security at the Danbury Fair.

John Leahy hired his own security for the fair that included the Pinkertons as well as the Danbury Fair Police force. He built headquarters for both and had patches, pictured here, designed for police uniforms. *Millie Godfrey.*

"Mostly we walked around making sure everybody was all right or asked if they needed help," she said. "We directed traffic, also."

DANBURY FAIR POLICE

"John W. Leahy wanted the Danbury Fair to be a safe and comfortable place for families to be," said Millie Godfrey. "Pinkerton and police activity helped keep it that way, and most fairgoers never saw what went on in the Fair Police Station."

Millie Godfrey's late husband, John, worked as a fairground police officer for twenty years, during which time he achieved the rank of deputy chief. Like most fair employees, John worked this part-time seasonal position in addition to his regular "day job," taking vacation time to work the fair.

THE GREAT DANBURY STATE FAIR

The Danbury Fair Police force in front of headquarters on the fairground in 1981. *First row, left to right*: Sergeant R. Fry, Sergeant C. Rees, Sergeant J. Joudy, Sergeant L. Robertson, Sergeant C. Zilinek, Sergeant G. Guertin and Sergeant R. Pawloski; *middle row*: Captain H Weyer, Deputy Chief J. Godfrey Sr., Chief S. Wilson, Captain J. Raymond, Captain C. Faust and Lieutenant R. Fuller; *standing*: Sergeant F. Richichi, Sergeant R. Foshay, Lieutenant F. Bishop, Lieutenant J. Wanat, Lieutenant Jturiano, Lieutenant J. Avanzato, Sergeant W. Englund and Sergeant C. Carr. *Photograph by Robert Mannion. Millie Godfrey.*

When their eldest son, Jay, was old enough, he joined his father on the Danbury Fair Police.

"John *loved* his job!" said Millie. "He worked the races every Saturday night, [and] he worked two weeks before the fair, during the fair and a week after the fair closed. Also in the summer when they had arts and crafts show."

Danbury Fair Police wore blue or white uniforms. The officers who wore white, like John, carried guns and were paid just a little bit more for this responsibility.

During Fair Week, John Godfrey began his days at 7:00 a.m. and often worked seventeen hours. Although the fair closed at 7:00 p.m., he had to wait for the accounting to be completed and then make a bank run.

People knew John Godfrey, deputy chief of the Danbury Fair Police, was serious about his work. He was one of a handful who carried a gun on the job. *Millie Godfrey.*

"Connecticut National Bank would open up so they could deposit; that might be close to midnight," said Millie. "There would be three or four cars loaded with officers with guns, like a parade, down to the bank. They used their own cars, and you never knew which car the money was in. Thank god, nothing ever happened."

Whereas John spent quite a bit of time at his desk in police headquarters during the fair, he was mostly in the pits during the Saturday night races.

"Sometimes the drivers got hot under the collar," said Millie, recounting a story of how one fellow in the pit mouthed-off at John. "He said, 'Yah, you feel pretty safe and pretty smart with that gun around your belly, don't you?' John wasn't afraid of anyone. He took off his belt and said, 'Now what do you want to do?'"

Millie, an avid race car fan who took her boys to the fairground's Racearena every Saturday, said the types of problems John handled at the fair were not "all that bad." People tried to sneak into the fair from the Orange parking lot, or someone was being a nuisance and had to be escorted out.

"He'd grab people out of the grandstand that were raising hell at the races," said Millie. "Or a drunk giving some of the carny men on the Midway a hard time. I don't want to give the impression we had a bunch of drunks over there—we didn't."

Millie calls the men who headed the Danbury Fair Police force "The Big Three." This included her husband, Chief Wilson and Captain Joe Raymond.

"Joe was on the microphone all day long—lost kids, announcements," Millie recalls. "If you've ever heard the announcement for the closing of the fair, it was his voice. It brings tears to my eyes."

THE PINKERTONS

"Most of the Pinkerton women were in the booths selling the ride tickets and working in front of the gates," said Judy Menegay Schoonmaker, who worked at the fair as a Pinkerton supervisor the last few years of the fair.

The Pinkerton men, she said, handled drunk and boisterous people at the races and took care of other situations that were "nonviolent."

"If it was anything more serious it was the Leahy police or the regular police who responded," she said. "It wasn't a real high-security job."

Judy, who grew up in Bethel, saw an advertisement in the newspaper and applied for the job. She received a badge and uniform of polyester blue pants, a lighter blue shirt and a coat. During fair week, Judy was one of at least seventy-five Pinkertons on staff.

Ticket-takers handled a substantial amount of money and it was Judy's job as supervisor to make sure that workers were safe and the money secured at the treasury building. John W. Leahy's wife, Gladys, was the treasurer of the Danbury Fair Inc., and was in the administration building from the time the fair opened until the accounting was finished in the evening.

"She was a petite woman. Very nice," said Judy. "I think it broke Gladys's heart that they sold the fair."

One day during Fair Week in the late 1970s, Judy's boss asked her if she had heard about the woman who had lost her car. He explained she had parked her car and gone into the fair, and when she came out, she couldn't find her car.

"She found a Pinkerton, and they ride around the parking lot in one of the little cars," said Judy. "The guy said, 'Oh there's your car.' The woman says, 'That's not my car; my car had a blanket in the back window.'"

The Pinkerton went over to the car anyway and tried her key. It unlocked the door but wouldn't start the car.

"They opened the glovebox, got the registration for the car," said Judy. "They called the guy up, who lived in Brewster, New York, and said to him: 'Did you go to the fair today?'"

The man said he had been to the fair that day. When the Pinkerton asked him where his car was, he responded it was in his driveway.

"No it's not," said the Pinkerton. "It's at the fairgrounds."

The man refused to believe him. Finally, the detective told him to go out and look at the license plate number of the car in his driveway. The man was dismayed to realize his mistake, mostly because had stopped on his way home to fill the car's gas tank.

During the race season, Judy worked as a Pinkerton on Saturday nights. She'd arrive at 5:30 p.m. and stand with the other ticket-takers at the gate, poised to make sure everyone who entered had a ticket.

"The Racearena sold advanced tickets the last few years of the fair," said Judy. "We ripped the tickets in half and let the people in,"

At 5:45 p.m., assistant general manager Fred Fearn would come out and stand behind the ticket-takers. He was the one to give the signal for the gates to open to advanced-ticket holders.

After the next wave of ticket holders were allowed through the gates and the clock approached 7:00 p.m., the ticket booths closed, and the Pinkertons moved to the grandstand.

"Each section in the main grandstand had a crossing gate," said Judy. "We'd close the gates and make sure nobody came down in front while the cars were going on the track."

At the end of race night, the Pinkertons took down and folded the twenty-by thirty-foot flag that hung out in the field.

16

At the Racearena

Midgets, Boats and Stock Cars

*There was once a lady who tried to sue the club and Fair management for a
supposed injury in the grandstand. She had purportedly broken a heel on her shoe
and gotten pregnant as a result. Mr. Leahy commented that that was original.
Most people came to see the races.*
—SNYRA: The Life and Times of the Southern New York
Racing Association

Racing and the Danbury Fair made a harmonious coupling for 112
years; one could not have existed for long without the other. The
fairground hosted a well-tended track, and the races brought in crowds and
much-needed revenue.

Although the track was at the same location all those years, it, like the fair,
had a variety of names: Danbury Fair Race Track, Danbury Fair Speedways
and Danbury Fair Racearena.

The earliest fairs featured one or two days of horse racing, and then the
races were daily. Auto racing was introduced at the 1909 fair. By 1918, a race
was scheduled each of the six days of the fair—horses the first five days and
automobiles the last.

When parimutuel betting was banned in Connecticut, interest in horse
racing waned. The last trotters ran at the Danbury fairground in 1940.

"They had big car racing there—the Indy car racers," said Irv Jarvis Jr.,
whose father had the job of finding entertainment for the fair.

Mario Andretti raced at the fairground early in his career. Randy LaJoie
also cut his teeth on the Danbury track before becoming a NASCAR

The Racearena was home to the Southern New York Racing Association from 1952 to 1981, when the fair closed. *From* The Newtown Bee.

champion. Racearena fans, however, didn't really care so much about all that. They were—and still are—just crazy about the local guys who were so intense and competitive on the track.

MIDGETS AND SPEEDBOATS

"After the trotters disappeared, and then the big cars left, there was a half-mile track with nothing going on," said Irv Jarvis Jr. "That's when my dad found out about the midgets and thought to build a smaller track inside the big track."

Midget Racing, the contest of small, open-cockpit, high-powered cars, thrilled visitors to the fairground starting in 1940. The first race was twenty-five laps on a one-fifth-mile track.

The midgets ran at the Racearena until 1964.

"A dispute about the number of races between John Leahy and the leader of the drivers, Dutch Schaeffer, resulted in the end of their appearance at the speedway," said Irv Jarvis. "Schaeffer ran an extra race for safety reasons after Leahy had told him no."

Speedboat racing was introduced at the fairground while midget racing was still in its heyday.

"They took the half-mile track and built a waterway and had speedboat racing," said C. Irving Jarvis Jr. "That was quite a mess. For one thing, they couldn't run the midgets and run the boats at the same time; the people of Danbury just didn't have the money to come out for both."

The Danbury Fair Watercourse, a racetrack-cum-moat, opened on Saturday May 20, 1950, with nationally known pilots racing in seven "thrill-packed" events. It was billed as the First Water Speedway of Its Kind in the United States. The speedway was thirty feet wide but only three feet deep and was rumored to have terrible leaks in its wooden sides.

The midget track was in the middle of the moat, so they had to build a bridge to get the cars to the track, Irv said. After the first season, Leahy decided to build his own boats, rather than hire the professionals who brought their boats from Florida.

"The boats had regular outboard engines—*very* noisy. They said they could hear them all the way to Newtown," said Irv. "People complained, especially the people in the neighborhood opposite the track."

Finally the police had so many complaints that they met with John Leahy and told him they were closing down the boat races.

"Leahy said, 'We've got everything booked for next week; let us run another show,'" said Irv. "They said, 'You run another show, and we've got to take you in.'"

Leahy ran the next race. And Irv, who helped that night as a starter lining everyone up, watched Leahy and his father get arrested by the police. Irv, his mother and sister, followed in the family car. The men were held for about two hours, he said.

"It was kind of a jolly thing," recalled Irv. "They didn't fine them, but they had to go through the process because the people probably would have raised hell if they didn't do something. So that was the last show of the speedboat races; it was the noise that killed them."

STOCK CAR RACING

Southern New York Racing Association (SNYRA), a nonprofit membership corporation, started looking for a permanent location shortly after it formed in 1948. A few years later, C. Irving Jarvis Sr. went to see the members race in Brewster, New York, and was impressed enough to make them an offer they found difficult to refuse.

"Dad said, 'You guys put on a hell of a show. If we build a track, will you come race with us?'" recalled Irv Jarvis Jr.

SNYRA started racing at the Danbury Fair's Racearena in 1952. The races drew a huge crowd during the summer and into the fall season. Like the speedboats, people said the event was so loud it could be heard in Newtown.

"But so many people loved the stock cars, there was no way you were going to stop them," said Irv. "They got great crowds."

The purse was a percentage of tickets sold for the event. Unofficial sources had told Charlie Mitchell, sports editor for the *Norwalk Hour*, that the purse was 40 percent.

"No track paid the purses Danbury did," wrote Charlie Mitchell in a feature for the *SNYRA: The Life and Times of the Southern New York Racing Association*. "A 20-lap feature would pay as much as $1,700 to the winner; twenty-five years later, long after the fair had closed, a 34-lap feature elsewhere in Connecticut paid $1,100 to $1,400."

The track was dirt when SNYRA first raced at the fairground, and ruts caused frequent accidents. The drivers were unhappy because they had costly repairs, and John Leahy was unhappy because the races ran late with delays due to clearing flipped cars from the track.

"It was fun to watch them but it wasn't good racing," said Irv. "Leahy had the track paved in one week—they never missed a meet."

The track had to be inspected by the state police every race week because it was under its jurisdiction, said Irv.

"They'd walk across the half-mile track and go to the midget track, walk around the track and go back to the office and that was it," said Irv. "It was more a formality at the time; they knew the track was in excellent condition."

When he was about fourteen, Irv had a friend whose father owned part of the food concession at the grandstand. They would spend the afternoon getting ice for the stand. Then his friend would take his father's pick-up truck while Irv took his great-grandfather's old orange Model T Ford, and they would race around the half-mile track.

"We were coming down the track—the home stretch—just as my father and the state police walked across it," said Irv, laughing. "My friend looked at me, and I looked at him. Then he hit my car and I took down about fourteen feet of railing. We thought: This is the end of our lives!"

Stock car racing at the Danbury Fairground became a community tradition. Fans described the Saturday night stock car races as the place to be.

"That was our Saturday night—you went to the races," said Judy Schoonmaker. "Friday night you might go bowling or out with your friends or out to dinner, but Saturday night you went to the races."

Because the same people would go to the races every week, it started to feel like "family," said Judy.

"We sat in the same place every week. We knew all the people around us," Judy said. "There were eight or ten of us just from Codfish Hill Road, in Bethel."

Between seven and ten thousand people filled the grandstand every single Saturday night during racing season. Drivers came from all over the area: Chick Stockwell was from Woodbury, Kenny Webb from New Milford and Don LaJoie from Norwalk. None of the drivers were professional racers. People rooted for the favorites, whether they were their childhood idol or the milkman.

"Kenny Canfield lived at the end of Hattertown Road in Newtown. He was always at the end," said race fan and dairy farmer Stephen Paproski. "We knew him; he used to deliver milk for us. He didn't go crazy; he didn't want to get in an accident. He was always at the end."

But one night, Stephen recalls a big wreck on the tracks and Kenny Canfield drove around the pile-up and did well.

Stephen was also a big fan of Chick Stockwell's because he went to high school with Chick's daughter and knew his son.

"He was a farmer; he didn't have the money all these other guys had," said Stephen. "He won quite a bit so everyone was happy to see him. I guess you had a favorite and you want your buddy to win all the time."

Judy Schoomaker and her husband were *huge* fans of Chick Stockwell's. The Schoonmakers were in the stands the night Chick beat out another favorite, Don LaJoie, to hit fifty wins. Although there was serious rivalry among the drivers and their fans (think Red Sox and Yankees), everyone in the grandstand stood up and shouted when car 151 passed the finish line.

"They could probably hear the whole stand in downtown Danbury: 'Let's Go Chick! Let's Go Chick!'" said Judy. "It was one of the greatest thrills of being at the fairground."

Chick Stockwell was voted favorite, or "winningest," driver by SNYRA fans year after year.

"That was one of his biggest thrills, being named favorite driver all those years," said Judy. "He was just an awesome person."

Millie and John Godfrey were big fans of Don LaJoie's. Laughing, she recalls that just as many people didn't like Don because he was winning all the time.

The Racearena track was *the* place to be on a Saturday night. Drivers were local guys who had a loyal fan base, like favorite Don LaJoie, pictured here. *Photograph by Robert Mannion. Millie Godfrey.*

"After Danbury closed, we never got racing out of our blood," she said.

Millie and her husband traveled to New Hampshire to see the generations of LaJoies race and visited them at their home in North Carolina.

"We just fell in love with this family," she said, "and followed their careers."

Stephen Paproski said his friends would always save him a seat at the Racearena because they knew he had farm work to do before he could leave for the evening.

"I'd get there halfway through the race. I'd get a tray of beer and go up to where my friends were," he said. "There was always a seat for me."

Bobby Marquis had the concession under the grandstand that sold food and beer. It was the only place selling food during the races. And the beer flowed freely.

"One guy in our section, Freddie, used to collect the [empty] beer cups, and he would put them up side down and stamp on them and everybody would cheer. If he didn't pop it, they would boo him!" said Judy Schoonmaker. "It amazes me that more people didn't get arrested for drunk driving back then after the races."

In the latest years of the fair, they closed the beer stand by a certain race, she said, so people had the chance to sober up.

"There were fights there all the time," said Stephen Paproski. "There was somebody who would *always* say something after the National Anthem—something not nice. I don't remember what they'd say. And all of a sudden you'd turn around and there were five guys holding him by his shirt!" he said. "Security was very tight there."

But even some things could never be anticipated or prevented, such as that which occurred Saturday, August 25, 1979. Millie Godfrey was in her usual box seat about halfway up the stands; Fred Fearn, who had become general manager when John Leahy died, was across the aisle from her.

"There was a terrible accident—a car flipped right under the starter's stand and flew up and hit our starter Ted Abbott. And he just flew out of the box onto the ground in front of the grandstand," said Millie. "One shoe came off Ted's foot and landed right up there in my box! That's halfway up

Starter Ted Abbott (inset) died when a car flipped under the starter's stand. The next week, all the drivers paid tribute to him. *Photograph by Robert Mannion. Millie Godfrey.*

the grandstand. I just sat there with it. I was in shock. Nobody had to be told; everybody knew he was gone."

In his memoir, *Racearena Memories*, Paul Baker called that "the saddest night." As announcer for the racetrack for twenty-three years, Paul was very friendly with Ted Abbott and knew how much the thirty-nine-year-old loved the races.

"Having been involved in racing for several years, Ted had told his mother if anything ever happened to him in racing, never to seek recourse from the club, track or sport," wrote Paul Baker. "While it is rumored she had been contacted by several persons suggesting she bring action, she honored Ted's wish and never did."

In his memoir, Paul Baker also recounted how tempers flared in the stands, in the pit and all around the metal announcing booth in the grandstand where he and scorer Jimmy Seeley were stationed.

"Once…an irate lady attacked. She kept swinging her purse at the back of my head," he wrote. "She didn't like what I said about Chick Stockwell in the race. The problem was that Chick wasn't even in the race, but I couldn't convince her. She kept swinging away."

After an accident when it took time for Mark Modzelewski to tow cars off the track, John Leahy got antsy and banged on the top of the roof of the announcing booth and shouted for Paul Baker to *do* something to fill the lull.

John Leahy also got stressed when his beloved bubble machines failed to work during the races. There were sixteen of them mounted on the rafters of the grandstand.

"As the music played, bubbles would come floating down on the crowd," wrote Paul Baker. "More often than not, the music wasn't very good, [and] the bubble machine didn't turn and failed to release the bubbles."

At the beginning of every race, for years without fail, the familiar voice of Paul Baker would broadcast throughout the grandstand:

"Good evening, ladies and gentlemen. On behalf of President John W. Leahy, Vice-President Fred Fearn, and the Southern New York Racing Association, this is Paul Baker bidding you welcome to stock car racing at the Danbury Fair Racearena, the East's most beautiful racing plant."

"Paul Baker was a heck of a nice guy," recalled Carl Tomanio, a big Racearena fan. "I can still hear him announcing: 'Number 72 from…' They would come shooting out of the pits and go around the track before they lined up for the race."

Rivalry between racers usually lasted just as long as the race. They were intense. They wanted to win. Once in a while, however, there was unexpected

Another unique Danbury Fair figure outside the Racearena. An earlier iteration has the track name across the starter's chest. *Photograph by Judy (Menegay) Schoonmaker.*

comic relief, such as the time Kenny Webb crashed through the back fence of the Racearena. He found himself in Dutch Village, so he drove through the village street and back up on the track.

Tradition had it that races were not held the Saturday before the fair opened and that the last race of the season was the Saturday after the fair closed. So Millie and John Godfrey's son, Jay, chose September 19, 1981, to be married so all of their fairground friends could attend the wedding.

"They goofed us up," said Millie. "Because the fair was closing down forever, they had the last race that day and a lot of people couldn't come to the wedding."

Millie, an avid fan and an organizer of the SNYRA reunions, and her husband, deputy chief of the Danbury Fair Police, managed to squeeze in one last glimpse of the stock car racing at the Racearena.

"We came back from the wedding reception in New York State and drove to the fairground," she said. "I'm in my gown, John in his tux, and we stood in Dutch Village and watched the last one-hundred-lapper."

17

A Fair No More

Death, Auction and Legacy

T'aint like Christmas. That lasts quite a spell. There will be a few sprigs of green hangin' 'round, and a few broken toys, and a few bits of candy…But the fair is different. It's a violent spasm when it's on, but when it's over it's done for. And it's over now—and ended.
—*Deby,* The Danbury Fair, *1894*

By the early 1970s, the first threads had started to unravel from the Great Danbury State Fair tapestry. Assistant general manager and "Entertainment King" C. Irving Jarvis had died, John Leahy's attempt to set up a foundation to perpetuate the fair after his death was thwarted and the dynamic millionaire was so sick he cast off his signature ringmaster's costume and, instead, wore a suit to the fair—when he was well enough to attend at all, that is.

But right before any of that happened, it seemed the Danbury Fair would go on forever.

The corporation had triumphed over the Danbury Airport's attempt to take by eminent domain some of its fairground parking, which would have greatly hindered attendance and, therefore, revenues.

In 1966, John Leahy, who had no children, established the Danbury Fair Foundation so the fair could continue after his death while providing an annual income for his favorite charities such as the Danbury Hospital. Within two years, Leahy had donated half of all the fair stock to the foundation. He also added a clause to his will so any remaining stock would funnel into the foundation.

When the Danbury Airport attempted to take some of the fair property by eminent domain, fair management and fans united to stop the action. *Photograph by Robert Mannion. Danbury Museum and Historical Society Authority.*

"I'm giving it all away," Leahy remarked in an October 12, 1968 *News-Times* article. "By giving it away, I keep it intact."

Leahy's goal was for the fair to run for "another 100 years—without any interference from the airport."

When Irv Jarvis died in 1969, Leahy tapped the manager of his fuel company, Fred Fearn, to be vice-president of the fair. Gladys's grandson Jack Stetson, who had worked at the fair his entire life, was given more responsibility and helped book concessions. That first October without Jarvis was the Danbury Fair's centennial.

In 1970, Leahy's well-considered plan for continuing the fair foundered. That year, the IRS determined no nonprofit could own more than 20 percent of a business. Leahy had to buy back—at increased value—all the stock he had donated during the past four years. He changed his will to exclude donations to the foundation.

After John Leahy died in 1975, concessionaires, SNYRA and "friends" purchased a five-thousand-pound stone with bas-relief by sculptor Dan Long to commemorate the fair manager. The monument is now on the Danbury Museum grounds. *From* The Newtown Bee.

Angry and unwell, Leahy never took any further steps to change his will to preserve the fair's future. News reports concur he intended to do so, but that oversight was the undoing of the Danbury Fair.

When John W. Leahy died in 1975, the route of his funeral procession went past the fairground. Robert Marquis, concessionaires, carnival operators and the Southern New York Racing Association chipped in to purchase a five-thousand-pound stone monument to the man who had turned a country fair into a wondrous experience filled with imagination and innovation.

Fred Fearn became president of the Danbury Fair and Jack Stetson, vice-president and secretary. Gladys Leahy, who was still treasurer of the corporation and worked on site during Fair Week, was the sole beneficiary of the trusts that comprised John Leahy's $7 million estate.

Real estate developers had been sniffing around the fairground for years; always they were rebuffed with a resounding, "No!" However, pressure to consider such offers increased after a reassessment of property in Danbury more than tripled the taxes for Danbury Fair Inc.

Fearn and Stetson had serious qualms about selling the fairground, but as trustees, they were mandated to do the best by the estate. Connecticut

National Bank and Gladys Leahy were the other trustees for the estate. In 1979, the trustees offered Wilmorite Inc., a Rochester, New York company, a $24 million option to build a regional mall on the 142-acre site.

Before a mall could actually be built, the Danbury Zoning Commission had to accept the proposal that the fairground property be changed from "light industrial" to "commercial" zoning. The wetlands were an issue. A few lawsuits ensued. But as history bears out, the zoning was changed in April 1981, and the last Danbury Fair was held that fall.

Concessionaires wore black armbands during the last Fair Week to express their grief about the fate of the 112-year-old event.

Jack Stetson was especially disappointed to realize he would never have the chance to be president of the fair, a position he had anticipated. The fair, he said in his 2003 oral history, "was the focus of our lives twenty-four hours a day, and we lived it all year long, planning for and working at it and seeing it happen every year."

Wilmorite Corporation exercised its option in the spring of 1982 and began to plan one of the largest malls in New England—one million square feet of commercial space—on what once had been the "Happiest Fairground."

"Johnny Leahy would roll over in his grave!" said Joan Ziegler, who knew the manager of the fair quite well.

The Danbury Fair Mall opened in 1986; it was the largest mall of its kind in New England. Three years later, the mayor of the city of Danbury James Dwyer was indicted on charges of accepting kickbacks from developers. He fought the charges and was acquitted.

"It's a shame the state or city didn't take that over," said Millie Godfrey.

She recalls fair managers opened the fairground during the off-season for corporate picnics, which provided additional income. The races alone were so popular, she said, and they provided a solid stream of income.

"What other event pulls in eight to ten thousand people on a Saturday night?" She shook her head. "I don't think we will ever know the real story."

THE AUCTION

Auctioneers D. Luther of New York grouped all the stoves, all the Indian figures, all the animal figures and all the signs and set them out on the 142-acre fairground. The auction ran for eight days in April 1982. The first days were unseasonably warm; the last day, it snowed.

The Danbury Fair auction ran eight days in April 1982. Collectors, amusement park owners and fairgoers who wanted one last piece as a memory attended. *Western Connecticut State University Archives.*

"The day we went to the auction it was a beautiful sunny April day, about sixty degrees," recalls Cathy Bronson of Maple Bank Farm in Roxbury. "It went down to fourteen degrees, and we had nine inches of snow three days later."

Cathy and her husband, Howie, bought flat wood and glass display cases that were eight by three feet and were peaked in the center. They used them as cold frames on the farm until weather rotted them.

"And we bought the Big Top tent; they actually sold it in pieces," said Howie, who uses the "strips" of canvas as tarps. "Every little section was so big it took about four really strong people to pick it up. One little piece rolled up."

Millie Godfrey, a lifelong Danbury resident and friend of John Leahy's, said she saw things at the auction she had never seen before in all her visits to the fair. She wasn't surprised by that, however.

"Every building had something on it, under it, over it," she said. "It was very sad to see these Indians lying on the ground that used to stand so tall. And Uncle Sam, Paul Bunyan."

Jack Gillette bought more than six hundred Danbury Fair pieces—twenty truckloads—to add to his Magic Forest Amusement Park in Lake George,

Familiar figures were grouped together for auction after the sale of the fair: animals, Indians, roosters, pixies and storybook characters. *Western Connecticut State University Archives.*

New York. At the auction, he met Art Provencher, the new owner of Bensons' Animal Farm in Hudson, New Hampshire, and they became friends.

"During the week, we would talk about which fiberglass figures he wanted to buy and which ones I wanted to buy," recalls Jack Gillette. "And if we both wanted the same one and nobody else was bidding, maybe we'd flip a coin so we weren't competing against each other. Save money, right?"

Animal figures he purchased at the auction inspired Jack Gillette to create a safari ride on a trackless train.

"I like the corniness of the fake stuff instead of the real animals," he said. "One of the horses I got from Danbury, I painted a purplish color and put a little sign out front that said: A Horse of a Different Color; many people catch the *Wizard of Oz* reference."

Although the auction dispersed the fair memorabilia, many fairgoers try to keep track of where some of it went. However, as Danbury Fair pieces are resold and repurposed, the trail of memorabilia has become hazier.

THE LEGACY

Fred Carly, a sports photographer who had grown up with C. Irving Jarvis Sr., enjoyed taking 16 mm silent films of the Danbury Fair every year. After the fair ended, Jarvis's son tried to locate the films to make a documentary. Jack Stetson, president of Leahy Fuel, had them, and together they interviewed people connected with the fair and produced the ninety-minute film, *The Great Danbury State Fair: America's Most Unique Fair; A Memoir*.

"I'd always wanted to do a documentary of the fair, especially after I lost my dad," said Irv Jarvis Jr., who is a retired producer.

Singer-songwriter Dave King created his music video with some of the fair film. His song, paired with the images, evokes an era gone by.

"Through Jack Stetson, Paul Baker got this pile of 16 mm film, and they wanted it all transferred to video," said Dave King, who worked with Paul Baker at Comcast. "I got set up in a spare closet in Comcast and had a video camera set up to shoot what I was projecting on the wall from the film."

Although Dave had never attended the fair, the images he saw during that week stuck with him—for twenty years. In 2009, he wrote a song based on the images in the film footage he had taped and made a video using some of this footage as well as film some friends had shot at the fair. He had a fair-going friend "fact-check" the song for accuracy.

Dave posted "The Danbury Fair" music video to YouTube and had a good response. But then his song was mentioned in a posting on the Facebook page Fans of the Great Danbury State Fair.

"It just blew up. It was crazy," Dave said. "I went to YouTube hourly, watching the numbers jumping by hundreds of views! That lasted for a week or two or three."

To date, the music video has had 14,500 hits.

After Dave King wrote "The Danbury Fair" song, his friend and avid racing fan Bob Brought Jr. pestered him to write a song about the fairground's Racearena. He did so and played his "Drivin' at the Racearena" at a reunion of the Southern New York Racing Association.

He had two different endings to the song, he said—one "sugar sweet" and another, that really hit a nerve: "Cause the Racearena's gone and it was loved by all / And now all we got is a stinkin' mall."

"The crowd just roared!" said Dave, laughing. "Just like *YEAH!* So I decided that was the one to use."

Elaine Lagarto set up the Facebook group Fans of the Great Danbury State Fair because of her own longing to see more photographs of the fair—few were available on the web—and, with the help of other former fairgoers, preserve the memory of the fair. She scanned all of her personal photographs, created a dedicated group and then invited her Facebook friends to join and contribute their images and stories.

"To my delight, within a few hours, I already had a few hundred members!" she said. "It was exhilarating to witness the rapid growth of the group. I was surrounded by people with similar feelings and memories—I was thrilled!"

To date, the group has posted 1,103 photos. Elaine spent a summer scanning and photographing the fair collection at the Danbury Museum and Historical Society Authority and offers members the link to that private album. She also searches the microfilm of local newspaper for articles about the fair and races.

With 3,674 members in every corner of the United States and even in Europe, Elaine believes people join the group because they still grieve the loss of the fair.

The Southern New York Racing Association hosts annual reunions of racecar drivers and fans. Shown here are singer-songwriter Dave King and "winningest" driver Chick Stockwell. *Photograph by Elaine Legarto.*

"Because of the Facebook fair group," said the founder, contributor and administrator, "there is, at last, a central place for all things Danbury Fair."

Another legacy of the fair is the annual reunion of the Southern New York Racing Association, which was first held in 2002. The Danbury event, first organized by Dan Evon, Gerry Dinnen and Millie Godfrey, attracts former racecar drivers and fans alike.

More than two thousand attended the first SNYRA reunion and its popularity continues to grow. Drivers who still had cars brought them and parked them in a line around the lot.

"This was a dream come true for fans, with all these fellows who used to be their heroes, that they watched on the track, and now they could touch them, talk to them," said Millie Godfrey, an avid fan herself, having missed only one race night between 1962 and 1981.

In addition to providing Racearena fans with annual meet-ups, the reunion raises money for charities, such as Paul Newman's Hole in the Wall Gang Camp for seriously ill children and their siblings.

In 2013, during what would have been Fair Week, Billy Michael and His Cavalcade of Stars presented the Great Danbury Fair Revue at the city's historic Palace Theatre. This evening of "music, memories, and more" that attracted three hundred people had an encore performance the following year.

WHAT HAS BEEN LOST

"The fair was the compass that gave Danbury a sense of direction and focus," said Elaine Lagarto. "It was not just the Leahy family running the fair every year. It really took a whole community to make the fair come alive."

The fair was also a rite of passage for locals, said Elaine. Included in her list of "firsts" that youth might experience at the Danbury Fair are going without an adult to the fair, going with a date, sneaking a kiss, working at the fair and, of course, that first amusement ride.

"The really lucky ones got to witness the fair through the eyes of their own child," said Elaine, who was pregnant with her first child when she attended the last fair. "To this day, it remains one my biggest heartbreaks that my own daughter never got to experience what I loved so very much."

Judy Schoonmaker also laments that her youngest daughter never had the opportunity to visit the fair.

Fair memorabilia is scattered all over the region in basements, barns, restaurants, garages and private collections. *Photograph by Catherine Vanaria.*

"It's a lost tradition," she said. "They don't know what they've missed. I've been up to the Big E, which is more commercial. This was more like Disney World."

Judy worked the last few years of the fair as a Pinkerton supervising the ticket booths and on the weekends at the Racearena.

"The last night sticks in my mind because nobody wanted to leave," she said. "Everyone wanted to ride the carousel for the last time. Everybody was sad; they didn't want it to end."

Jill Austin vividly recalled the last fair. "I think everyone had the same feeling: I can't believe this is it," she said. "That fair really put Danbury on the map."

Farmers, as well as 4-H and other youth groups in the area, no longer have the opportunity to show the animals they raised without traveling a distance, said Alyce Block, longtime Farm Bureau board member and committee chair.

"Other fairs are thriving, drawing huge crowds," said Alyce, who would travel with her husband to fairs in New York and Maine after the

Danbury Fair closed. "The average person has lost a lot by not having the Danbury Fair—the sewers, the quilters, the people who did crafts."

Arlene Yaple, superintendent of the Big Top for thirty-five years and news correspondent for *The Newtown Bee,* wrote a piece for the newspaper in 1982 during what would have been Fair Week.

"Not only is the pleasure that was given to fair visitors gone forever, but the comradery that developed between those working behind the scenes has been lost," she wrote. "Break-up nights ended with the traditional 'see you next year,' never 'goodbye.'"

The mall adopted the fair's name, placed a new carousel in its food court and hung photographs of the event on its walls. But many fairgoers and race fans have such bitter feelings about the development of the property that they have never stepped through the doors of the mall.

"In the hearts of many," wrote Arlene Yaple, "a day at the mall will never replace the gaiety, happiness and enjoyment of eight hours on the fairground that was so much a part of Danbury and the lives of many."

"If my dad and Leahy were alive, that fair would still be going," said C. Irving Jarvis Jr. "They would never have ended that fair; that would have gone on and on."

Selected Bibliography

Bailey, James M., and Susan Benedict Hill. *History of Danbury, Conn., 1684–1896.* New York: Burr Print. House, 1896.

Baker, Paul. *Paul Baker's Racearena Memories.* N.p.: self-published, 2010.

Burpee, Charles W. *Burpee's The Story of Connecticut.* New York: American Historical, 1939.

Commemorative Biographical Record of Fairfield County, Connecticut, Containing Biographical Sketches of Prominent and Representative Citizens, and of Many of the Early Settled Families. Chicago: J.H. Beers, 1899.

Connecticut: A Guide to Its Roads, Lore, and People. Written by Workers of the Federal Writers' Project of the Works Progress Administration for the State of Connecticut. Boston: Houghton Mifflin, 1938.

Connecticut State Library and Archives, Hartford, Connecticut.

The Connecticut Tercentenary, 1635–1935, and the Two Hundred and Fiftieth Anniversary of the Settlement of the Town of Danbury Which Included the Society of Bethel, 1635–1935: A Short Historical Sketch of the Early Days of Both Towns and Program of Events. Danbury, CT: Tercentenary Committee, 1935.

Conner, John Wayne. "A Comparison of the 1940 and 1969 Danbury State Fairs," 1971. Truman A. Warner Collection, Western Connecticut State University Archives.

Danbury, Connecticut and Its Attractions. Danbury, CT: W.A. Blissard, Printer, 1923.

The Danbury Fair. Danbury, CT: Danbury Medical Printing, 1894.

Danbury Fair Cook Book. New Haven, CT: O.A. Dorman, Printer, 1888.

Danbury Fair, October 1, 1947. RG 069:146, James L. McConaughy Papers, box 5, envelopes 68 and 79, State Archives, Connecticut State Library.

Danbury Historical Society and Museum Authority Archives, Danbury, Connecticut.

Devlin, William E. *We Crown Them All: An Illustrated History of Danbury.* Woodland Hills, CA: Windsor Publications, 1984.

SELECTED BIBLIOGRAPHY

Four Cities and Towns of Connecticut: Historical, Biographical and Commercial. New York: Acme Pub. & Engraving, 1890.

Ganio, John P. "Origins of the Danbury Fair," June 9, 1969. Truman A. Warner Collection, Western Connecticut State University Archives.

Governor's Day at the Danbury Fair, October 7, 1981. RG 005:037, Office of the Governor: William A. O'Neill (1980–1991) records, box 330, folder 445, State Archives, Connecticut State Library.

Historical Sketch of Danbury and the Danbury Fair. Danbury, CT, 1890.

Hurd, D. Hamilton. *History of Fairfield County, Connecticut with Illustrations and Biographical Sketches of Its Prominent Men and Pioneers.* Philadelphia: J.W. Lewis, 1881.

News-Times, Danbury, CT.

Newtown Bee archives, Newtown, Connecticut.

New York Times, New York, NY.

Porter, Edwin, S. *A Rube Couple at a County Fair.* Video. New York: Edison Manufacturing Co., 1904.

Redding Remembered. John Reed Middle School, Redding, CT, Redding Oral History Project, 1979–[1983?].

SNYRA: The Life and Times of the Southern New York Racing Association. Flemington, NJ: Program Dynamics, 1996.

Stetson, Jack. "The Danbury Remembers—Conversations with a Community: Danbury History Project Oral Histories." Interview by Theresa Buzaid. OH 001, box 1, tape 12, Western Connecticut State University, October 8, 2003.

Stetson, Jack, and Irv Jarvis. *The Great Danbury State Fair: America's Most Unique Fair; A Memoir, 1869–1981.* Video. Danbury, CT: Film Fair Productions, 1997.

Stilgoe, John R. *Common Landscape of America, 1580 to 1845.* New Haven, CT: Yale University Press, 1982.

Truman A. Warner Papers, 1940–1997, Western Connecticut State University Archives.

Typescript titled "The Great Danbury State Fair," undated [by William Devlin submitted to Paulette Pepin?]. Danbury's Third Century Research Collection, MS 058, box 1, folder 29, Western Connecticut State University Archives.

Wilson, Lynn Winfield. *History of Fairfield County, Connecticut, 1639–1928.* Chicago: S.J. Clarke, 1929.

Zimmermann, Andrea. *Eleanor Mayer's History of Cherry Grove Farm: Three Generations on a Connecticut Farm.* Newtown, CT: Newtown Historical Society, 2005.

Zimmermann, Andrea, Mary Maki and Daniel Cruson, eds. *Newtown Remembered: Continuing Stories of the 20th Century.* Newtown, CT: Newtown Oral History Project, 2010.

Zurlo, Lewis, "Danbury Fair, Liquidation Auction." Western Connecticut State University Archives. http://archives.library.wcsu.edu/omeka/items/show/3017.

Index

INDEX

INDEX

INDEX

About the Author

Andrea Zimmermann is a writer, photographer, artist and librarian with a keen interest in local history and preservation. She is the author of two other books, *Eleanor Mayer's History of Cherry Grove Farm* and *The Case Files of Detective Laszlo Briscoe: True Crime in Newtown, 1889–1933*; contributor to *Letters from Sandy Hook–Newtown to the World*; and editor of *The Remarkable Huntingtons* and three volumes of oral histories. Andrea has been a librarian for eighteen years. She was a features writer for *The Newtown Bee* before becoming a freelance journalist writing for the *New York Times* Connecticut Weekly section and regional magazines. She established and was director of the Newtown Historical Images Archive, a Newtown Historical Society project to digitize and preserve more than three thousand photographs that document life in Newtown

ABOUT THE AUTHOR

between 1880 and 1950. She has taught college courses on English and publicity. Andrea has a master's of arts in English and masters of library and information sciences. Her freelance photographic work appears in regional magazines, such as *New England Boating*. She is currently writing a mystery novel. Andrea makes her home in Newtown, Connecticut, with Bill Brassard Jr. and their springer spaniel Libby.